RAND NATIONAL DEFENSE RESEARCH INSTITUTE

From Negative to Positive Stability

How the Syrian Refugee Crisis Can Improve Jordan's Outlook

Ben Connable

For more information on this publication, visit www.rand.org/t/RR1069

Library of Congress Cataloging-in-Publication Data is available for this publication.
ISBN: 978-0-8330-9087-4

Published by the RAND Corporation, Santa Monica, Calif.

Cover image: AP Photo/Mohammad Hannon

Preface

In late 2013, the Marine Corps Intelligence Activity (MCIA) asked the RAND Corporation to examine how the United States might improve its support to Jordan. Jordan is a critical U.S. ally, and Jordan's continued stability and support are deemed essential to ongoing coalition activities against the Islamic State and to broader efforts to improve stability in the Middle East. RAND researchers identified both risk and opportunity in the Syrian refugee crisis. This report presents findings from a year of research conducted in the United States and Jordan and presents analytic forecasts intended to support U.S. government analyses and policy decision-making. This report was aided by the expertise of the reviewers, Rochelle Davis, Georgetown University, and Barbara Sude, RAND.

This research was sponsored by the Office of the Secretary of Defense and conducted within the Intelligence Policy Center of the RAND National Defense Research Institute, a federally funded research and development center sponsored by the Office of the Secretary of Defense, the Joint Staff, the Unified Combatant Commands, the Navy, the Marine Corps, the defense agencies, and the defense Intelligence Community.

For more information on the RAND Intelligence Policy Center, see http://www.rand.org/nsrd/ndri/centers/intel.html or contact the director (contact information is provided on the web page).

Contents

Figures and Table

Figures

Table

Summary

This report describes the late-2014 stability of the Hashemite Kingdom of Jordan and examines how the Syrian refugees are likely to affect Jordan's long-term stability. The key finding from this research is that the Syrian refugee crisis, while challenging in the near term, offers opportunities to improve Jordan's long-term economic, social, and security outlook.

Research for this report was completed in late 2014. Some significant events and trends in 2015 may shed light on RAND's original findings and forecasts. These include the murder of the Royal Jordanian Air Force pilot Muath Al-Kasasbeh by the Islamic State in January 2015, the slow but significant growth of the Syrian refugee population in Jordan, the increasing challenges in funding refugee support activities in Jordan, the kingdom's growing role in regional stability activities, and the deteriorating security situation in Jerusalem. However, none of these 2015 events appears to negate assessments and forecasts made in late 2014. Most prominently, the assessment that Jordan would remain stable through 2015 has so far borne out. Unfortunately, so did the assessment that any failure to aggressively fund Jordan's refugee support programs would, in turn, erode opportunities to leverage the Syrian refugee situation to improve Jordan's long-term stability. Recent reporting indicates that more refugees are impoverished in 2015 than in 2014. Further research is needed to assess the impacts of wavering donor support in 2015.

The remainder of this report is presented as written in late 2014, with minor inclusive edits.

As of late 2014, many American and Jordanian experts believed Jordan to be stable and unlikely to collapse from internal unrest or external invasion, at least through the end of 2015. However, some observers believed that the kingdom's stability depended more on popular reluctance to confront the government rather than popular support for the government. One expert interviewed for this report called this dynamic negative stability, or stability driven by fear of unintended consequences rather than positive support. By properly managing the refugee crisis, the Jordanian government can influence its population toward a more lasting, optimistic, and robust internal stability.

While Jordan is stable, it suffers from a range of existing and emerging challenges. Syrian refugees pose several challenges and stability risks to the government of Jordan (GoJ), but it does not appear that any of these constitute an existential threat to the overall stability of the Hashemite Kingdom. There are three key areas of concern, each of which is addressed in this report: economic, social, and physical security. The risk across each of these categories is manageable, and, if present integration trends continue, the refugees might have a positive effect on both the Jordanian economy and society. In early December 2014, the GoJ submitted a $2.87 billion plan to respond to the Syrian refugee crisis through 2015. If fully funded, this plan has the opportunity to improve employment, service delivery, and infrastructure across Jordan. Furthermore, the Syrian refugee crisis in Jordan and the concomitant support from allied states have helped to cement Jordan's most important international relationships and firmly establish the kingdom as a vital regional safety net for potentially disruptive refugee populations. Ultimately, it might be possible to successfully integrate tens, if not hundreds, of thousands of Syrians into Jordanian society with an overall net positive impact.

Specific near- to mid-term economic impacts of the refugees will be mixed but at least partly positive. Some Syrians will remain dependent on aid and will demand national and international resources for several years. Even with increased aid there will be some unremitting strain on Jordan's already-inadequate national budget. However, many enterprising and technically skilled Syrian workers have already entered the Jordanian labor force, and in many cases they have started their own productive businesses. While some Jordanians have complained about Syrian refugees crowding the labor market, the GoJ, several nongovernmental organizations (NGOs), and many private citizens have taken positive steps to both integrate Syrians into the economy and take advantage of their technical and entrepreneurial skills. If properly encouraged and officially sanctioned, the Syrians might boost Jordan's economic output and, if their employment can be formalized, the GoJ tax base.

The social impact of the refugees will also be mixed, but the negative effects are likely to be localized to areas of high "off-camp" refugee concentrations, such as Irbid and Mafraq. While some Jordanians resent the refugees or are fearful of their economic or security effect, many others have welcomed the Syrians into their communities and have helped them to integrate into Jordanian society. Some Syrians who fled to Jordan after the 1982 Hama massacre and are now Jordanian citizens have also provided considerable assistance to refugees. Many religious organizations, including the Jordanian and former Syrian Muslim Brotherhood, have also provided aid that has helped sustain the Syrian refugee population.

All of these local efforts have been supplemented or supported by extensive international aid and by official GoJ programs, and, to some extent, the Syrians' social integration is dependent on the continuation of these aid programs. If aid dwindles and the Syrians place a greater strain on the Jordanian economy, then resentment and friction between Jordanians and Syrians might increase. However, because the Syrians are entrepreneurial and because many appear motivated to remain in Jordan indefinitely, time is on the side of stability. As the Syrians find economic stability, they will be less vulnerable to the loss of aid, and therefore less likely to present a drain on Jordanian society.

Because the Syrian refugee population is large and for the most part unobserved by either NGO or government reporting agencies, in theory it might represent a security threat to the GoJ. However, there was little evidence as of late 2014 that threats from the Syrian refugee community are significant or existential. Reported increased support for Al-Nusra Front and the Islamic State in such cities as Ma'an, Jordan, might present opportunities for militant Syrian refugees to integrate with and enhance the strength of Jordan's relatively limited yet dangerous extremist population. The extremist threat to the GoJ should not be taken lightly, nor should the possibility that Syrians might support the oppositionist—yet so far mostly peaceful—Jordanian Muslim Brotherhood movement. However, even if the Muslim Brotherhood is providing aid to the Syrian refugees, it does not necessarily follow that these Syrians will support the Muslim Brotherhood or support political or violent anti-GoJ activities.

There will almost certainly be incidents of individual Syrian refugees, or small groups of refugees, posing security threats to Jordan. There is open-source evidence of activity in Jordan by the Al-Qa'ida–linked Al-Nusra Front and the Islamic State, and some of this might be linked to Syrian refugees; recent arrests of Islamic State associates in Jordan highlight the potential for danger. However, because the GoJ has maintained a fairly moderate tone in its dealings with the Syrian government and with various threat groups, it has not established itself in opposition to either pro-Assad or anti-Assad militants. And while some Syrian refugees might be extremists, and some Jordanians are extremists, recent data show that most Jordanian citizens reject violent extremism and do not wish either an external or internal force to depose their government. Instead, they want government reform, better services, improved minority protection, and security. Therefore, Syrian extremism is unlikely to translate into increased Jordanian extremism or into a serious threat to the stability of the GoJ. It is important to note that as the Islamic State continues to morph into a regional and global organization, the scope of the Islamic State extremist threat will expand beyond the Syrian refugee population to include Iraqis, Indonesians, Filipinos, Gulf Arabs, and others, many of whom can transit Jordan or influence Jordanian citizens through electronic media.

Any forecast of complex social, economic, and security environments and events should be read with caution. This is particularly true of mid- to long-range forecasts that offer estimates of probability ranging out beyond a few months. This forecast is vulnerable to unpredicted shifts in projected trends, highly improbable but dangerous or positive "black swan" events, or simply inaccurate or misleading information. Much depends on the future of the conflicts in Syria and Iraq, as well as on the willingness of the international community to continue to support the GoJ. However, based on available information in late 2014, it appears likely that Syrian refugees in Jordan will, at worst, present a continuing expense within the GoJ budget and anger some Jordanians, and, at best, the refugees might enhance Jordan's economy and society. Many problems will be localized and therefore manageable at the state level. The security threat posed by Syrian extremists and criminals is real but also likely manageable with existing GoJ assets and existing levels of U.S. support.

CHAPTER ONE

Introduction to the Status of Syrian Refugees as of Late 2014

This report describes the stability of Jordan as of late 2014 and provides insight into the status and effect of the Syrian refugees in Jordan. The report then presents forecasts of the effect these refugees might have on Jordanian stability. This introductory chapter provides a brief overview of Jordan and issues with Jordanian stability, a summary of the Syrian refugee situation as of late 2014, and a description of the research methodology and report structure.

Between 2011 and late 2014, fighting associated with the Syrian civil war forced nearly 3 million Syrian civilians to flee their homes.[1] Some of these Syrians are now internally displaced persons (IDPs), while others have fled to Turkey, Lebanon, Iraq, or further abroad. Hundreds of thousands of Syrian refugees fled south to the Hashemite Kingdom of Jordan. This influx of new refugees into Jordan has strained Jordan's already overburdened budget, and the presence of the refugees has generated economic and social disturbances. These increasing tensions have led many observers of Jordan to question whether the Syrian refugees pose a serious, or perhaps even existential, threat to the government of Jordan (GoJ).

Geographic Orientation and Syrian Refugees as of Late 2014

The Hashemite Kingdom of Jordan is a constitutional monarchy with an elected parliamentary government; this elected body has some control over decisionmaking and the execution of policy.[2] The current King of Jordan is Abdullah the Second (Abdullah II).[3] Figure 1.1 is a map of Jordan, which shows its difficult geopolitical situation; as of late 2014, Jordan borders two countries in the midst of violent civil wars (Syria and Iraq), both Israel and Palestine, and Saudi Arabia. Jordan shares maritime space with Egypt—another country suffering internal turmoil—across the Gulf of Aqaba, to the south. The relatively porous border between Jordan and Syria is approximately 379 kilometers, the distance between Washington, D.C., and Manhattan.[4]

---

[1] United Nations High Commissioner for Refugees (UNHCR), 2014c.

[2] The degree to which Jordan's monarchy is constitutional and representative is often debated; this is perhaps true of all constitutional monarchies. King Abdullah II has spoken about this subject on several occasions in the past decade. For information on Jordan's constitutional monarchy, see Hamid and Freer, 2011; U.S. Central Intelligence Agency, 2014; GoJ, undated; Ryan, 2014; Koprulu, 2014; O'Toole, 2014; and Yom 2014a, 2014b.

[3] King Abdullah's full name is Abdullah bin Hussein bin Talal bin Abdullah bin Hussein bin Ali. He is listed as an author under this name in the references.

[4] U.S. Central Intelligence Agency, 2014.

Figure 1.1
Jordan Overview

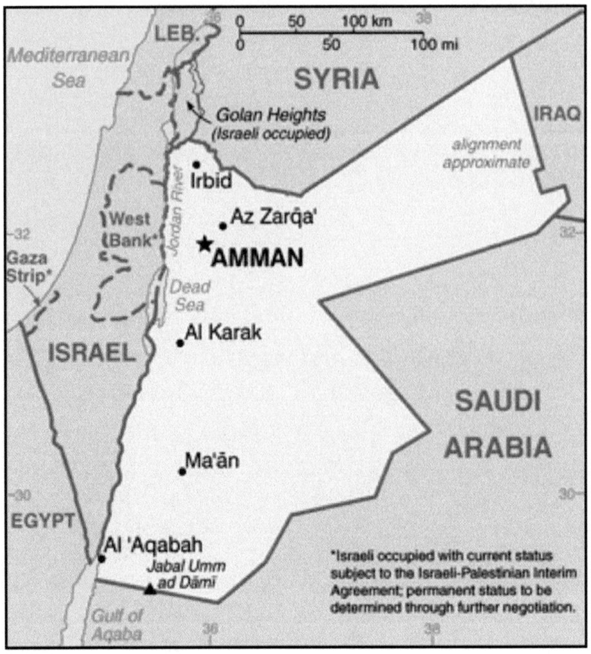

SOURCE: U.S. Central Intelligence Agency, 2014.
RAND *RR1069-1.1*

Figures 1.2 and 1.3 depict the northern and southern portions of Jordan, respectively. Figure 1.2 shows the Jordanian cities of Irbid and Mafraq, both of which are located just south of the major Syrian conflict zone of Dara'a.[5] Ar Ramtha, Irbid, and Mafraq are often the first—and last—stops for Syrian refugees entering Jordan; both Irbid and Mafraq figure prominently in this report. The major city of Zarqa lies between Mafraq and the capital, Amman, to the south. Many of the poorer Syrian refugees appear to live in Zarqa. Amman is located farther south and is denoted by a black star. Roads between Irbid, Mafraq, and Amman are highly trafficked bituminous asphalt roads, which offer easy, if sometimes congested, movement from the border cities to the capital.

Figure 1.3 shows the southern portion of Jordan. This area is much less densely populated than the north; most of the populated areas are along the Desert Highway and the King's Highway to the west (running roughly in parallel with the Jordan River, north to south). Ma'an, a commercial and industrial city in the south-central desert, has been a focal point for periodic antiregime, extremist, and even some separatist activity since at least the late 1990s. Aqaba, Jordan's only port city, is a commercial transit hub. Some Syrian refugees are working in the tourism industry in Aqaba, although the exact number of Syrians in the far south is unknown.[6]

---

5 Irbid, Mafraq, Zarqa, Amman, and other areas are also referred to as *governorates*. These political boundaries are broader than the city boundaries and include other, smaller, municipalities.

6 UNHCR reports approximately 3,000 registered Syrians living in Aqaba Governorate from month to month in late 2014 and early 2015. However, this number does not reflect unregistered Syrians or even all registered Syrians who might be living in the south for temporary employment in the tourist industry. UNHCR, 2014d.

Figure 1.2
Northern Jordan

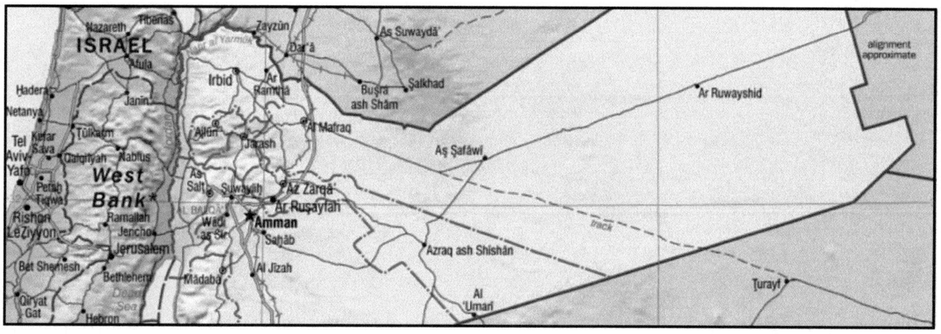

SOURCE: U.S. Central Intelligence Agency, 2014.
RAND *RR1069-1.2*

Figure 1.3
Southern Jordan

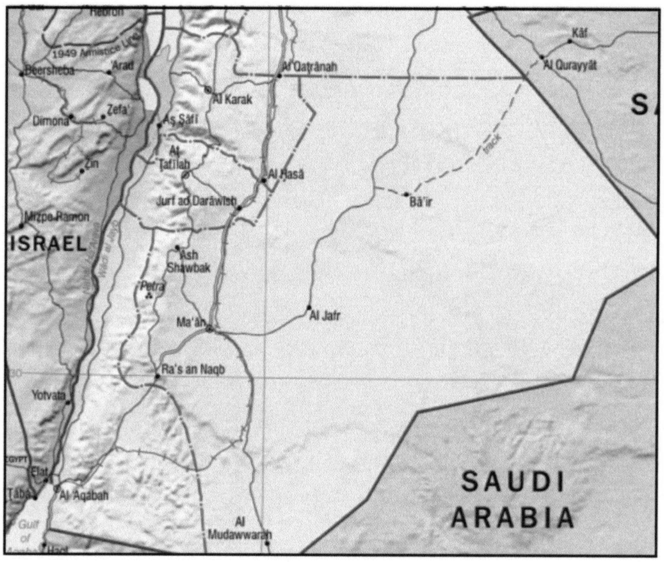

SOURCE: U.S. Central Intelligence Agency, 2014.
RAND *RR1069-1.3*

Syrian Refugees in Jordan: Late 2014

As of December 2, 2014, the UNHCR registered 618,615 Syrian refugees as having entered Jordan, of whom only 96,968 lived in three camps—Zaatari (81,776), Azraq (11,197), and the Emirati Jordanian Camp (3,995)—leaving the remaining 521,647 officially registered Syrian refugees in Jordanian communities—from Irbid and Mafraq in the north to Aqaba in the south.[7] There has been a slight decline in official camp population and a slight increase in over-

[7] UNHCR, 2014f. See Ward, 2014; and Serrato, 2014, for analyses of camp conditions and UNHCR and United Nations Development Programme (UNDP) procedures.

all registered refugees since August 2014, but the changes are insignificant.[8] The total number of unregistered Syrian refugees in Jordan is unknown, and it is not clear that all registered refugees remain within Jordan's borders. Some experts believe that there might have been as many as 800,000 registered and unregistered Syrian refugees in Jordan as of late 2014.[9] For purposes of empirical accuracy and commonality with other publications, this report uses the UNHCR's August 2014 figure of 600,000 as a rough estimate of the overall number of Syrian refugees in Jordan.[10]

As of late 2014, Zaatari was by far the largest of the three government-sanctioned Syrian refugee camps. Official estimates of the population in Zaatari are only estimates, and the actual population of the camp might fluctuate by thousands, or even tens of thousands, of people over the course of a week. RAND interviewed individuals who worked in the camps and who had conducted site surveys of Zaatari; these interviewees stated that people enter and exit the camp with minimal restrictions. It is not known whether these procedures were tightened in late 2014.[11] Zaatari gains a great deal of attention because it is the busiest camp and the most accessible, and because, by population, it is technically one of the largest cities in Jordan. Zaatari has also become something of a testing ground for a wide range of refugee management and protection programs, some of which have proven successful enough to migrate to other camps. However, while Zaatari is a relatively large refugee camp, the vast majority of Syrian refugees in Jordan live on the economy.

Reporting differs on the locations of these out-of-camp (or off-camp) refugees, but the distributions appear to be relatively stable between 2012 and 2014. Approximately one-third (approximately 171,600) lives in Amman Governorate, in the center of the country; another third (approximately 158,400) lives in Mafraq Governorate, in the northwest; and the others are concentrated in Irbid Governorate (approximately 144,000) and Zarqa Governorate (approximately 67,200), located just north of Amman.[12] There are scattered concentrations further south and east. The left part of Figure 1.4 shows where the UNHCR conducted home-visit surveys of off-camp Syrian refugees. While this late-2013 distribution does not represent an empirical estimate of actual distribution of off-camp refugees, it generally aligns with other estimates and is also useful to convey the concentrations and distributions of population in each governorate. The right part of Figure 1.4 shows August 2014 distributions of refugees—both in and out of refugee camps—across all of Jordan. Note the smaller distributions in Karak, Tefilah, Ma'an, and Aqaba, to the south.

---

[8] Comparing the data in UNHCR, 2014e, and UNHCR, 2014f, shows that the collective registered camp populations declined by 3,544, or about 3 percent, during this period. Since registration and the tracking of registered persons is an inexact process, it seems logical that there might be as much as or more than a 3-percent error in official data month to month. This assumption is reinforced by interviews with Jordanians who have worked in the largest camp, Zaatari.

[9] This number emerged in two interviews with subject-matter experts (SMEs). There does not appear to be any empirical evidence to support or refute these estimates.

[10] UNHCR, 2014e. This number includes only those refugees from recent fighting (2011–2014) and not from previous periods of conflict in Syria.

[11] RAND conducted interviews with a number of experts and refugees in Jordan. To preserve anonymity, each interviewee is referred to by a number and the date of the interview is provided. Interviewees 4 and 6, November 18, 2013.

[12] Precise registration figures are provided in UNHCR, 2014f, but all head counts and locations are necessarily estimates. The UNHCR does not have the capability to track all registered Syrian refugees in Jordan.

Figure 1.4
General Population Distribution of Syrian Refugees in Jordan

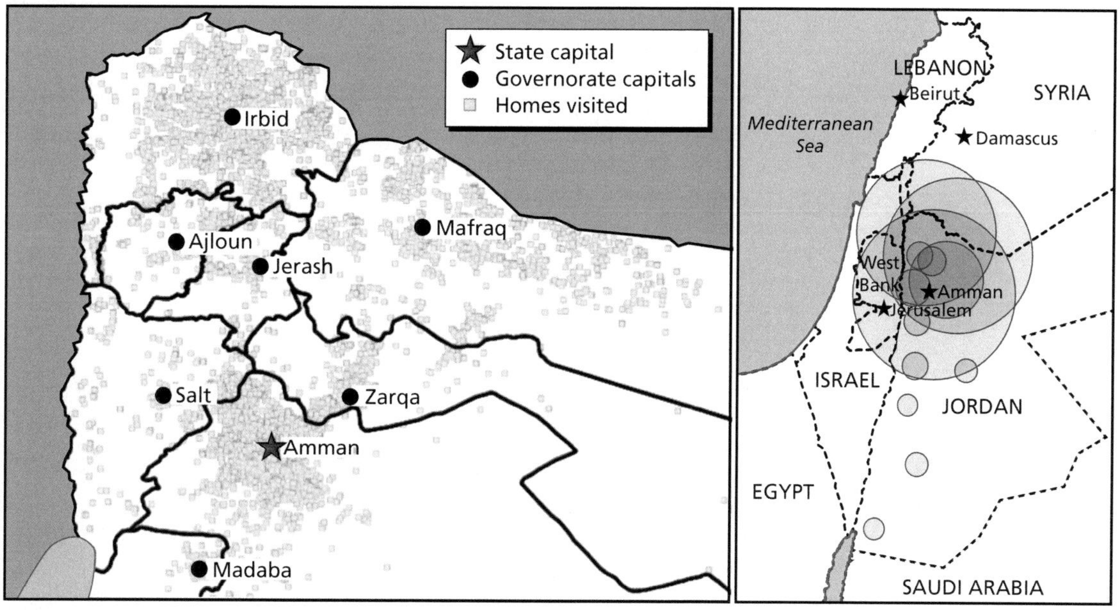

SOURCES: UNHCR, 2013; UNHCR, 2014e.
NOTE: The left side shows where the UNHCR conducted home-visit surveys of off-camp Syrian refugees in 2013. The right side shows the distribution of refugees—both in and out of refugee camps—across all of Jordan, as of 2014. Karak, Tafileh, Ma'an, and Aqaba are represented by the four bubbles running generally north to south below Amman and along the Jordan Valley to the west.
RAND *RR1069-1.4*

UNDP reporting shows that in such places as Irbid, along the Syrian border, the refugees might make up nearly half, and in some cases more than half, of the local population. For example, in November 2013, they reportedly made up 57 percent of the population of New Taybeh municipality: approximately 4,000 out of 7,000 people. Even in larger communities, such as New Ramtha, the Syrians might have made up as much as 40 percent of the population (40,000 out of 100,000) in late 2013.[13] A UNHCR study showed that about half of Syrian refugee income is derived from humanitarian assistance and charity, while about one-third of income is derived from labor conducted in Jordan (e.g., a Syrian refugee receives pay for writing code for a technology firm in Amman or building homes in Irbid).[14] A significant number of Syrian refugee children do not attend school, although both the GoJ and various humanitarian groups are working to rectify this problem.[15]

The degree to which off-camp Syrians are integrated within the economy varies by functional sector (e.g., water, sanitation, housing). While perhaps 50 percent of Syrian households are led by unemployed parents and are therefore vulnerable and perhaps more willing to return, at some point, to Syria, about 90 percent of all off-camp Syrians rent space in some kind of resi-

[13] UNDP, 2013c, chart 25.

[14] UNHCR, 2013.

[15] See, for example, UNHCR, 2013, p. 5.

dential facility.[16] This means that approximately 450,000 of the estimated 600,000 off-camp and on-camp Syrian refugees in Jordan live in a permanent (typically rented or donated) facility.[17] Most refugees (80 percent or more) have access to adequate clean water, sanitation, and other services.[18] Therefore, while perhaps 200,000 Syrians in Jordan live in impermanent or inadequate conditions, 400,000 live at least at the level of low-income Jordanians. This means that approximately two-thirds of the Syrian refugees in Jordan are not only off camp but also at least partly integrated into the Jordanian national and local government services systems.

Methodology

The analysis and forecasting in this report are derived from an inductive 12-month (late 2013 to late 2014) research effort conducted in the United States and in the Hashemite Kingdom of Jordan. The primary research question posed by the sponsor was: How will the influx and persistent presence of Syrian refugees in Jordan affect the country's long-term stability? The purpose of this research question was to help identify threats to Jordanian stability to inform U.S. decisionmaking in support of this critical U.S. ally.

To answer the research question, the RAND principal investigator assessed (1) the current stability of Jordan in 2013–2014, (2) the vulnerabilities associated with potential instability, (3) the status of Syrian refugees in Jordan, and (4) the status of other refugee groups in Jordan to help shed light on the Syrian refugee situation. This effort involved a review of extant literature (e.g., books, older periodicals with current relevance), which included a qualitative meta-analysis of 16 studies and surveys related to Jordanian economic, social, and security issues.[19]

Research also included a three-month, week-by-week (12 iterations), open-source media analysis effort that leveraged both English- and Arabic-language news material, an Arabic-language analysis of social and political commentary on YouTube, semistructured interviews with 18 U.S. and Jordanian experts, and analysis of existing survey data on Jordanian refugee, economic, social, and political issues.[20] All of these sources helped identify trends in Syrian

[16] UNHCR, 2013, p. 49. These numbers vary by region and might have changed as of late 2014, although they are generally substantiated by other local surveys cited in this report. Housing types in the UNHCR report include basements of single-family apartments or houses, commercial spaces, apartment units, houses, self-made structures, mud houses, prefabricated houses, and tents.

[17] I address tent camp domiciles later in the report.

[18] UNHCR, 2013.

[19] These are UNDP, 2013a, 2003b, 2003c; Hafferkamp, 2014; UNHCR, 2013, 2014a; Alafi and Alfawaeer, 2014; Shahateet, Al-Habashneh, and Al-Majali, 2014; Khrawish, 2014; K. Gharaybeh, 2014; Jabbar and Zaza, 2014; Althbutat and Ghawanmeh, 2014; Serrato, 2014; United Nations Women, 2014; Ibrahim, Sauer, and Yassine, 1976; CARE, 2012; Olwan and Shiyab, 2012; Hansen and Eriksson, 2013; REACH 2014a, 2014c; International Labour Organization (ILO), 2012; and Mercy Corps, 2012.

[20] Sources are identified in the references and are too numerous to list here. We used several variations of semistructured interview protocols for different interview pools and individuals. Questions centered on issues of stability and instability in Jordan, the Syrian refugee populations, and other refugee populations, as well as on such broader regional issues as the ostensible Sunni-Shia' split across the Middle East; some questions informed rather than centered on the Syrian refugee issue.

refugee activities in Jordan, perceptions of Syrian refugees from various Jordanian subnational populations, and a range of security trends relevant to Jordan's stability.

Analyses and forecasting were derived from the data and SME input obtained during the period of research. The analyses and forecasts presented in this report represent the inductive research findings and the SME assessment of the principal investigator (the author), who traveled to Jordan five times to conduct interviews, make observations, and have numerous informal conversations with Jordanians across the country and at all levels of society. The timelines for forecasts are

- near term: immediately through one year
- mid term: one year through three years
- long term: three years and longer.

Citations are provided for all findings, while forecasts in the main body of the report are separated from the analysis, in distinct sections. This separation is intended to avoid conflation of findings with forecasts, as well as to provide other researchers and analysts the ability to draw on empirical analysis without the incorporation of SME forecasting. The forecasting is intended to help the sponsor build follow-on analytic efforts and to support mid- to long-term decisionmaking regarding Jordan and the Middle East. Where appropriate, forecasts include recommendations for additional analyses.

A note on forecasting: Forecasting is an inherently risky and uncertain process. It is possible to reduce, or perhaps distribute, risk by using approaches based on experts' consensus, such as like RAND's Delphi method or any model that incorporates expert opinion from multiple sources.[21] The research team was unable to identify SMEs on the Syrian refugee problem in Jordan who had equivalent knowledge of the refugee situation and also the economic, political, social, and security situation, *and* who were available to participate in an expert forecasting exercise.[22] Instead, forecasts in this report incorporate input, and independent forecasts, from the 18 interview subjects. Therefore, the forecasts represent both the expert interpretation of the author and input from expert interviewees in the United States and Jordan. The construction, formatting, and descriptive language used in the forecasts are informed by documents with estimative analysis from the U.S. Central Intelligence Agency and the Director of National Intelligence, as well as several academic and practitioner articles.[23]

---

[21] These approaches typically ask a group of SMEs to answer a series of questions about a single question or set of narrowly focused questions. There are typically several iterations of questions, as either a scenario is described and evolved in phases or SMEs answer, debate, engage, and then readdress each question. The results of these efforts are distilled, or perhaps concentrated, versions of multiple SME analyses on a single issue. Some of the models involve computer-assisted simulation or data processing. See, for example, Helmer, 1967.

[22] There was insufficient structured data and research resources to apply a highly structured approach, such as agent-based rational choice stakeholder models or any computer-aided efforts.

[23] These include, but are not limited to, Kent, 1964; U.S. Director of National Intelligence, 2007a, 2007b; Partee, 2007; and Friedman and Zeckhauser, 2012, 2015.

Organization of This Report

Descriptive analysis, findings, and forecasts are presented in three categories: economic, social, and security. Chapter Two describes the current stability of Jordan and, through a subjective expert analysis of strategic challenges, lays the groundwork for the more specific analyses and forecasts in the following chapters. Chapter Three addresses economic issues in Jordan and the current and forecasted impact of Syrian refugees on the Jordanian economy. Chapter Four addresses social and political issues in Jordan and the current and forecasted impact of Syrian refugees on Jordan's social structure and political stability. Chapter Five identifies current security risks and forecasts how both small groups of Syrians and the larger population of displaced Syrians are likely to affect Jordanian stability and security. The final section of the report presents a cumulative analysis and a mid- to long-term forecast for the impact of Syrian refugees on Jordan's stability, as well as an assessment of "black swan," or highly improbable yet dangerous or positive, events that might have a serious impact on stability.

CHAPTER TWO

Assessment of Stability and Strategic Challenges: Late 2014

This chapter presents a general assessment of Jordan's stability as of late 2014 and offers a summary forecast for 2015. It then describes several strategic challenges described by SMEs in literature and interviews. These general and specific assessments are intended to serve as a guide for the examination and forecasting of Syrian refugee impact. This chapter sets a baseline for the assessments and forecasts of economic, political, and security impacts in the following chapters.

Jordan's Stability as of Late 2014

Jordan remained stable throughout the Arab Spring period that began in 2011 and ebbed at the end of 2012. As of late 2014, Jordan was socially, economically, and physically stable, despite the many challenges assessed in this report.

Summary forecast: It is likely that the kingdom will remain whole and stable throughout at least 2015. There are no imminent internal threats that would unseat the Hashemite regime or that would generate widespread and uncontrollable social violence.[1] While external unrest on Jordan's northern and eastern borders is extreme, as of late 2014, it does not appear that there are imminent external threats that would either threaten Jordanian government control over the kingdom or lead to a loss of Jordanian territory to external entities. Nonetheless, there are a number of black swan events that might undermine Jordanian stability. Several of these are listed in Table 6.1.

Security from External and Internal Threats

As of late 2014, Jordan is generally secure from external military threats. Jordanian Armed Forces (JAF) units defend the northern and eastern borders from direct assault by conventional or organized guerrilla forces, and the new unified border security element is steadily improving its efforts to control the complex microterrain of small wadis, hills, and rural villages along the border with Syria.[2] Individual infiltration likely occurs on a daily basis, particularly in

[1] This assessment reflects interview data for this project, as well as an assessment of extant literature. The most-recent data input for this assessment was from discussions with U.S. and Jordanian experts in Amman and Washington, D.C., in late September and early October 2014.

[2] See Qojas, 1999, for a JAF officer's perspective on the physical challenges of border security, and Oksam, 2013, for a summary of the Jordan Border Security Program. Also see Sharp, 2014, pp. 3–5; and Barhoumeh, 2014.

the more densely populated areas around Irbid and Mafraq, but the border with Iraq is more secure.[3] The Royal Jordanian Navy and Marines and the JAF's Southern Command Army forces secure the southern borders with Israel and Saudi Arabia, as well as the critical port facilities in the Gulf of Aqaba.[4] Increased American military presence in Jordan might, now or in the future, offend some Jordanians, but the presence of an operational headquarters element (U.S. Central Command Forward—Jordan) and increased theater security cooperation activity appears to be serving the dual purpose of demonstrating U.S. support to Jordan and increasing the confidence of senior Jordanian leaders.[5]

Internal security was of greater concern in late 2014, but most experts believed that internal violence could be isolated or controlled at least through 2015. Reports of increased support for regional Islamic extremist groups, such as the Islamic State and Al-Nusra Front, have increased from late 2014, with some particularly troubling reports emanating from the south-central city of Ma'an.[6] Extremist banners have been spotted in the city, and there have been several incidents of violence ostensibly related to extremist activity.[7] Ma'an has been a continual center for protest and resistance in Jordan, with major flare-ups of activity in 1989, 1999, and 2002.[8] In one recent incident, a shooting at a university in Ma'an led to a major dispute between "East Bank" (or regime supporter) Huweitat tribesmen and Ma'ani citizens; this eventually resulted in a disruption of north-south traffic along the critical Desert Highway.[9]

However, some experts question the degree to which the disruption in Ma'an is connected to the Islamic State and Al-Nusra Front. While there are almost certainly some hard-core Salafist jihadists in Ma'an and surrounding areas, the number of extremists is unknown, and their support even within Ma'an is immeasurable.[10] The incident with the Huweitat tribesmen was disruptive but more about local relationships and tribal issues than extremism or instability. Interviews with Ma'anis (citizens of Ma'an) in a July 2014 *Asharq Al-Awsat* article reveal disputes over extremist presence and the political manipulation of Ma'an's image as an extremist-controlled city.[11] One expert on Jordan stated:

---

3 Formal assessments of border security are typically classified. This general assessment is derived from open-source reporting and from discussions with U.S. and Jordanian officials.

4 This finding derives from direct observation by the author in mid-2013, early 2014, and late 2014, as well as discussions with Jordanian military officers.

5 This assessment is derived from discussions with U.S. military officers, Jordanian military officers, and a survey of news articles associated with the deployment of the small contingent of U.S. forces to Jordan.

6 See, for example, Abuqudairi, 2014; Al-Daameh, 2014; Booth and Luck, 2014; and Su, 2014. This point is also derived from several interviewee responses from interviews conducted throughout 2014.

7 Abuqudairi, 2014. Protesters in the summer of 2014 carried banners calling Ma'an the "Fallujah of Jordan," in an exaggerated comparison to the Iraqi city that was a focal point for insurgent activity from 2004 through 2007.

8 See Ryan, 1998; and Schwedler, 2002.

9 Interview 1, November 17, 2013.

10 Polling in Ma'an is particularly difficult due to the ongoing security crackdown, and also due to the reluctance of some Ma'anis to engage with outsiders. This assessment is derived from informal conversations with polling experts in Jordan. Native Arab reporters have good access in Ma'an and have generated insightful stories, but even collectively these reports do not rise above the level of anecdotal evidence.

11 Al-Daameh, 2014.

> Ma'anis know that protests and riots don't work. They understand that these are expressive actions, and they want them to echo in Amman. They use the black flag to get the attention of the palace because they feel they are being forgotten.[12]

This expert's assessment might or might not be accurate, but it does offer a plausible alternative to reports that Ma'an is now a hotbed of Islamic State and Al-Nusra activity. Further, while Ma'an is a focal point for some overt social disruption, it is also a hub for internal and cross-border criminal activity. It is unclear to what degree the troubling behavior in Ma'an is extremist or criminal in origin. It is also unclear whether this perceived disruption in Ma'an will spread across Jordan. While social disruption in Ma'an can spread, or perhaps be reflected elsewhere in the country, as of late 2014, it does not appear that extremists in Ma'an have been able to significantly influence other population centers or threaten the regime.

Unrest in Ma'an and various antigovernment protests in Karak, Tafileh, Salt, and Amman during 2014 likely have far more to do with social and economic concerns than with support for antiregime extremists.[13] Several recent surveys taken by different polling companies using disparate methods and questions have all highlighted concerns with social justice, political representation, employment, and the impacts of expatriate groups, such as the Syrian refugees. A February 2014 survey report by Madison Springfield Incorporated stated: "The vast majority of respondents considered pressing economic, political and social grievances far more important than the threat posed by Islamist extremism."[14] The same survey revealed greater concern over economic and social disparities than with terrorism, as well as low support for Islamic extremism. Political, social, and economic issues are addressed in this and the following chapters.

Political Turmoil and the Impact of the Arab Spring

As of late 2014, Jordan was politically stable, particularly in comparison to neighboring states. The 2011 Arab Spring generated protests in Jordan but did not lead to a widespread open revolt against the GoJ. Based on a range of expert assessments, as well as observations and analysis by the author, there does not appear to be any immediate threat of countrywide instability.[15] This assessment is made with the understanding that no experts forecasted the rapid overthrow of the regime in Tunisia, or the speed with which peaceful demonstrations in Syria, Ukraine, and other nations have morphed into existential threats to long-standing regimes since 2011. In late 2014, all nation-states in the Middle East appeared more fragile and susceptible to local and regional unrest than in previous decades.

Jordan has gone through periodic waves of internal political instability, dating back to the protectorate period in the early 1920s. Of these many historic waves of unrest, only the 1970 Black September attacks by the Palestine Liberation Organization (PLO) had the potential to completely destabilize the country. Yet throughout these waves of instability, Jordanians have

---

[12] Interview 15, September 7, 2014.

[13] Interview 15, September 7, 2014.

[14] Duboisse et al., 2014b. This survey consisted of 40 interviews and 857 survey questionnaires across northern and central Jordan.

[15] See Ryan, 2014; Krasner, 2014; and Yom, 2014a. Hansen and Eriksson, 2013, also provide a good in-depth analysis of Arab Spring dynamics in Jordan.

typically sought to redress grievances through active yet relatively peaceful demonstrations and political action rather than force. The Jordanian Muslim Brotherhood is often described as the "loyal opposition" because, unlike its Egyptian counterpart through 2011, the Jordanian Muslim Brotherhood worked within the system to bring about reform.[16] Until recently, nearly all Jordanians refrained from criticizing the King and instead focused their opprobrium on the parliamentary government. But this enduring redline began to erode in 2011. While Jordan is politically stable, growing discontent among East Bank Jordanians—the bedrock of Hashemite rule—is generating concern among Jordanian experts and allies. Perhaps the clearest manifestation of this discontent is Hirak (the Movement).

The Jordan expert Sean L. Yom charted the development of Hirak as an organized political movement and later as a generic descriptive term used by journalists and pundits to explain increasing East Bank discontent with the GoJ and with the Hashemite Kingdom.[17] Protests by East Bank Jordanians were almost unheard before the 2011 Arab Spring. East Bankers tended to benefit most directly from government employment and largesse, and they viewed themselves as having the greatest stake in Jordan's long-term stability.[18] They were therefore reluctant to show disloyalty to the Hashemites. Yom and other experts argue that this firm position eroded slowly during the past two decades as East Bankers perceived that they were being ignored in favor of Palestinian businessmen, refugees, and other non–East Bank constituencies.

As the Arab Spring erupted in early 2011, approximately 40 disparate grassroots movements emerged across Jordan. First rural and then urban East Bank protesters demanded political and social reform in mostly peaceful but often boisterous protests. Protesters crossed two long-accepted redlines in Jordanian politics: They openly criticized the King, and they openly suggested changing the royal line of succession to shift control away from Abdullah II and his son.[19] In Yom's view, these original, grassroots Hirak protests represent a potent threat to Jordanian stability:

> In historical perspective, the Hirak represented the most dangerous threat to authoritarian order due to the redlines they crossed *combined* with the East Bank tribal forces they represented—so much so that while the regime largely tolerated the protests of the Islamists and other urban opposition, it sought to crush the far smaller and dispersed rural protests of the Hirak.[20]

This assessment was reinforced through interviews with other experts. Yet many interviewees also stated that, since 2011, the protests have settled and the original Hirak movements are diluted or dissipated. Yom traces the decline of Hirak and attributes it to aggressive internal security measures and the inability to organize above the submunicipal level.[21] Regional instability has also taken a toll on antigovernment zeal. One interviewee stated, "Jordanians look around the region and see chaos, and they don't want it. They believe the King is better than

---

16 Robinson, 1997; Robbins and Rubin, 2013; Althbutat and Ghawanmeh, 2014.

17 See Yom, 2014a; and, particularly, Yom, 2014b.

18 Yom, 2014b; and interviews 17 and 18, November 24, 2014.

19 Yom, 2014b, p. 235.

20 Yom, 2014b, p. 235; emphasis in the original.

21 Yom, 2014b, pp. 245–247.

civil war."[22] This same interviewee, a Jordanian expert on political and social movements and unrest, referred to this phenomenon as *negative stability*: The population avoids direct confrontation with the government because it fears instability. Palestinian Jordanians, many of whom are quite unhappy with the political and social conditions in Jordan, might also be motivated by negative stability. One expert on Palestinian sentiment described the kind of resignation that Yom and other interviewees described among some East Bankers:[23]

> A lot of Palestinians are resigned; they are not happy with Hamas or the Palestinian Authority, so they look around and say, there's a lot of corruption in Jordan and oppression, but it's not bloody. They say fine, I'd rather live with the status quo . . . than live with attacks in the streets or airplanes bombing buildings. They look to Iraq. The King in Jordan will not send in tanks or bomb.

The instability caused by the Arab Spring has made any and all forecasting in Jordan more difficult and less reliable. For example, few would have forecasted that in late November 2014, the leader of the Jordanian Muslim Brotherhood would be arrested for making inflammatory statements against the United Arab Emirates.[24] Forecasting stability and instability in Jordan depends in great part on accurately assessing the balance between legitimate and motivating grievances and the *negative stability* sustained by ongoing civil collapse in neighboring states.

Water Shortages Contribute to Economic and Social Unease

Jordan faces a growing water crisis that threatens to cause endemic shortages by 2020.[25] In 1999, King Abdullah II stated: "Our water situation forms a strategic challenge that cannot be ignored. . . . [D]rinking water remains the most essential and the highest priority issue."[26] The reasons for this severe shortage are multifarious, but they include population growth, inadequate management, crumbling or inadequate infrastructure, and politically motivated overuse. Normal population growth among East Bankers and permanent Palestinian citizenry—even without the influx of refugees—portends steady increases in demand, even as supply falls or remains even in various regions of Jordan.[27] About 93 percent of normal rainfall in Jordan is lost to evaporation, but recent year-on-year reductions in rainfall attributed to climate change have further depleted groundwater supplies.[28] Scott Greenwood and others argue that the GoJ misallocated or overused water to supply political patrons, exceeding normal usage and depleting water supplies. This mismanagement has reportedly contributed to nearly 75-percent drops in well levels in some farming areas. Al-Ansari, Alibrahiem, Alsaman, and Knutsson describe

---

[22] Interview 1, November 17, 2013.

[23] Interview 14, February 20, 2014.

[24] Sweis, 2014.

[25] For example, see Al-Ansari, Al-Oun, et al., 2013; Al-Omari, Salman, and Karablieh, 2013; Namrouka, 2013a; Al-Ansari, Alibrahiem, et al., 2014; Alqadi and Kumar, 2014; and Greenwood, 2014.

[26] See UNHCR, 2014b.

[27] Altz-Stamm, 2012, and others point out that tourism also places significant demands on Jordan's water resources; tourists and the growing hospitality industry should not be overlooked in calculations and assessment of resources.

[28] Al-Ansari, Alibrahiem, et al., 2014; also see, e.g., Alqadi and Kumar, 2014, p. 323.

how up to 46 percent of water might be lost through poor or poorly controlled infrastructure, such as broken pipes or illegal rerouting in Mafraq and, likely, in other places.[29] All of these existing and mounting problems have been exacerbated by the influx of Iraqi and Syrian refugees.

Officials and experts see three possible solutions to the water crisis: (1) find, purify, and make available sufficient existing potable groundwater; (2) use "virtual water," or the importation of such water-intensive products as wheat, to reduce agricultural demands on Jordan's own water resources; and (3) dramatically increase the importation of desalinated water into Jordan.[30] The first option seems increasingly untenable as supplies drop and demand increases; indeed the GoJ acknowledges that existing ground resources are "over abstracted."[31] Several experts deem the use of virtual water untenable, and the water-resource expert Dennis Wichelns argues that there are conceptual and practical flaws with applying virtual water models to solve national-level water shortages.[32] This leaves increased desalination as the only realistic option to solve Jordan's water crisis.

King Abdullah II, the government, and donor states recognize these problems, and the GoJ has implemented or supported a wide range of policies and programs to try to avert a crisis. In 1988 Jordan established the Ministry for Water and Irrigation to try to tackle regional and local water problems, and in 2009 Jordan issued a comprehensive water strategy.[33] The "Red to Dead" desalination project is now central to hopes of solving or significantly assuaging Jordan's water deficits. This project, to be completed by 2018, will pipe desalinated water from the Red Sea into the Dead Sea and further north and east, thereby replenishing the Dead Sea and giving Jordan access to water along the agricultural belt on its western border.[34] If successful, the Red to Dead project and ongoing infrastructure improvements would help reverse Jordan's declining water resources. But progress will be blunted if Jordan's population—including long-term refugees—continues to grow at current rates.

Economic and Financial Dependencies

As of late 2014, Jordan was fiscally stable, but only with the considerable and continuing assistance of foreign donors, lenders, and grantors. In 2013, the U.S. government provided the GoJ with approximately $1 billion in aid. Funding in 2014 also amounted to approximately $1 billion. In 2013, approximately $300 million of this aid went to foreign military sales, $180 million to U.S. Agency for International Development (USAID) projects, and about $200 million went to direct grants. The United States also supports Jordan with sizable loan guarantees.[35] In late 2011, five members of the Gulf Cooperation Council pledged a total of $5 billion to the

---

29 Al-Ansari, Al-Oun, et al., 2013; also see Greenwood, 2014.

30 See, for example, Ministry of Water and Irrigation, 2009, undated; Altz-Stamm, 2012; Alqadi and Kumar, 2014; and Al-Ansari, Alibrahiem, et al., 2014.

31 Ministry of Water and Irrigation, undated. Also see Alqadi and Kumar, 2014, p. 324.

32 Wichelns, 2010.

33 Ministry of Water and Irrigation, 2009.

34 Ministry of Water and Irrigation, undated.

35 Interview 5, November 18, 2013.

GoJ; some of this money has already been transferred to the kingdom's treasury.[36] And at least tens of millions of dollars flow into Jordan from other donors in numerous smaller grants or loans. Experts disagree as to whether the GoJ is dependent on external funding to pay public-sector salaries, but most data and analyses cast doubt on the ability of the government to pay civil or military employees without some external support.[37] Therefore, under current conditions, the central pillar of the state—the public sector—can stand only if Jordan continues to receive considerable year-on-year aid packages.

This is not to say that Jordan is completely dependent on public-sector employment to sustain its economy. The kingdom also has a robust business and banking sector. Palestinian Jordanians have demonstrated exceptional entrepreneurial skills, capitalizing on a relatively highly educated and skilled labor market and ready access to both registered and unregistered foreign workers.[38] A wave of Iraqi refugees and repatriated Jordanians from Kuwait in 1991 helped spark an extended period of business development, particularly in Amman. Jordanian banks own a significant portion of government debt.[39] This is positive for the banking sector and has helped Jordan establish itself as an emerging financial center. However, because banks are so tied to government debt, there is little remaining capital to fund private companies.[40]

Official statistics and expert estimates of economic conditions reveal some enduring weaknesses in the Jordanian economy and some early trends that may warrant greater concern. Data vary in quality and availability, but trends from 2010 through 2014 suggest that unemployment hovers at about 13 percent and poverty at about 14 percent.[41] The Congressional Research Service suggests that unofficial unemployment might be as high as 25–30 percent, and poverty might be as high as 30 percent of the population.[42] Verifying official data is difficult, so both official statistics and expert estimates are less reliable than similar data from countries with long-standing statistical programs.[43] Nonetheless, even a low estimate of 13 percent unemployment suggests that there is a sizable population of adult Jordanians who are liable to resent refugee job seekers. Reports on tax revenue vary, but government revenue from tax collection is low. A 2012 USAID report estimates that tax revenue amounted to 15.2 percent of gross domestic product (GDP)—a percentage consistent with many developing nations but far below some Western nations—but one expert believed that only 2 percent of Jordanians consistently pay income tax.[44] The GoJ heavily subsidizes low-income households and some con-

---

[36] See, for example, Al-Rawashdah, 2012a, 2012b; and Numan, 2013. This chapter also references interview 5, November 18, 2013.

[37] In an informal discussion, one Jordanian expert firmly disagreed that Jordan was dependent on foreign aid or loans to sustain public-sector salaries.

[38] Interviews 17 and 18, November 23, 2014.

[39] Interview 18, November 23, 2014.

[40] Interview 5, November 18, 2013.

[41] See, for example, Al-Saraireh, 2014; and World Bank, 2014. The GoJ Department of Statistics lists the unemployment rate at 12.6 percent for 2013. See Department of Statistics, 2013a, p. 40.

[42] Sharp, 2014, p. 11.

[43] Close assessments of Jordanian economic statistics indicate significant gaps between official data and a clear holistic picture of the formal and informal economies. UNDP, Jordan Economic and Social Council, and the Spanish Agency for International Development Cooperation, 2010; and Department of Statistics, 2013a.

[44] USAID, 2013, p. 4; interview 2, November 18, 2013. Most Western nations see approximately 25–40 percent tax revenue as a percentage of GDP.

sumer commodities, although these subsidies have been cut in recent years.[45] Jordan also faces a growing youth bulge. Nearly 70 percent of the population is under the age of 29 and nearly 40 percent is under the age of 15. Data for 2012 indicate that youth ages 15–24 make up more than 35 percent of the total workforce.[46] All of these statistics and expert estimates indicate an underlying potential for instability, although other regional governments were able to maintain stability for decades while exhibiting even less desirable economic trends.[47]

In recent polling (late 2013 to late 2014) Jordanians express a great deal of concern over lack of economic opportunity or demonstrate a perception of economic inequality. The 2013 World Bank country poll found that job creation, economic growth, and equality of opportunity were important priorities for Jordan.[48] Economic concerns were dominant in some studies. For example, late 2013 to early 2014 polling, interview, and focus group research by Madison Springfield Incorporated indicated that high percentages of Jordanians believed that high prices, unemployment, lack of economic opportunity, and pay gaps were serious problems.[49] In that study, economic concerns outweighed fears of political unrest or extremist violence.

However, there are some indications that Jordanian *perceptions* of economic weakness exceed indicators. In the Madison Springfield Incorporated study, 86 percent of respondents believed that unemployment was "a major problem" in their local area, but only 16 percent of these respondents claimed to be unemployed.[50] And 27.7 percent of respondents in a World Bank study thought that job creation was a priority, but the demographics of the study suggest that nearly all of the respondents were themselves gainfully employed.[51] And while the Congressional Research Service suggested that actual unemployment might greatly exceed official estimates, several of the interviewees engaged for our study also suggested that perceptions of economic weakness exceeded realities.[52] Regardless of whether perceptions match, exceed, or undervalue actual economic shortfalls, these perceptions seem to be influencing Jordanians' views of Syrian refugees. See Chapter Three.

Existing Refugee and Nonnational Worker Populations

As the Syrian civil war erupted in 2011, Jordan was already host to approximately 2 million registered Palestinian refugees, the vast majority of whom are now Jordanian citizens. That number remained consistent as of late 2014. Approximately 370,000 of these Palestinians live

[45] Interview 2, November 18, 2013; "Subsidy Cuts, Higher Housing Costs May Keep Inflation in Jordan High," 2014; and Solomon and Bassam, 2013.

[46] Strategies Policy Research, 2013; Department of Statistics, 2013a.

[47] For example, Egypt subsisted for more than six decades without a major revolt while routinely registering very poor economic performance and appearing at the bottom of most stability indices. See the Global Observatory website (Global Observatory, 2012).

[48] World Bank, 2013. Respondents were able to choose three options: 27.7 percent chose job creation/unemployment, 23.8 percent chose economic growth, and 8.5 percent chose equality of opportunity. Job creation/unemployment ranked as the third-greatest priority, behind public-sector governance/reform and energy.

[49] Duboisse et al., 2014b, p. 13.

[50] Duboisse et al., 2014b, p. 13.

[51] World Bank, 2013, pp. 4–9.

[52] Sharp, 2014, p. 11.

in official camps.[53] Most Palestinians are fully integrated into Jordanian society, although there are still rifts between some East Bank Jordanians and some Palestinian citizens.[54] And Jordan has also hosted perhaps hundreds of thousands of Iraqi refugees since 2003; the total numbers over time and as of late 2014 are widely disputed.[55] The UNHCR estimates that approximately 24,000 Iraqis live in camps in Jordan, as of mid-2014.[56] Many Iraqi refugees are also integrated into Jordanian society, and many of these refugees have been able to sustain themselves without aid.[57] Many Iraqi refugees were repatriated, but current instability in Iraq may reverse that trend.

Official acceptance of both Palestinian and Iraqi refugee populations has been mixed. While Palestinians are integrated into Jordanian society and serve in the GoJ, there is some evidence that they are restricted from attaining the most-influential positions in government or the armed forces.[58] Palestinian Jordanian business people are some of the most successful in the country, but there is still some (perhaps uneven) lingering discontent at all Palestinian Jordanian socioeconomic strata. And while Iraqis have contributed to the Jordanian economy and have kept a relatively low profile in social and business sectors, there is growing concern that additional refugees from recent fighting in Iraq will exacerbate Jordan's problems.

There are also hundreds of thousands of foreign national (*nonnational*) laborers in Jordan at any one time. Most of these are Egyptians, although there are also Filipinos, Bangladeshis, Sri Lankans, Indonesians, and others. An official 2012 report identified 335,000 nonnational workers officially employed in Jordan that year. However, estimates of unofficially employed people are much higher.[59] One expert stated that, as of 2014, there were likely 800,000 Egyptian laborers working in Jordan.[60] While there is no reliable way to determine the actual number of unofficial laborers in Jordan, the vast majority of these laborers—90 percent, according to an ILO report—are illiterate, and only 0.53 percent of the officially tracked nonofficial labor population had a bachelor's degree, as of 2012.[61] For the most part, these laborers are poorly paid, and they are strictly limited to manual activities. They have little hope for social or economic advancement and likely remit most of their salaries. In some cases, these nonnational workers are ill treated by their employers. There have been scattered protests against oppressive labor practices, but the fear of expulsion likely mutes most protest activity.[62] The GoJ is acutely aware of these problems and has taken measures to improve workers' rights and protections, as

---

53 United Nations Relief and Works Agency, 2014.

54 For example, see O'Toole, 2014; Yom, 2014a, 2014b; and Robinson, 1997, 1998.

55 For example, see Chatelard et al., 2008. Figures range from 450,000 to approximately 24,000. None of these is accurate, since there were no real efforts to count and register Iraqi refugees entering Jordan during the early stages of the U.S.-led war in Iraq. Many Iraqis actively avoided registration because of issues with valid passports, visas, taxes, and security. These same issues are likely to affect Syrian refugees, but there is no empirical analysis showing how these legal concerns might dissuade Syrians from registering in Jordan.

56 See, for example, UNHCR, 2014d.

57 Interviewee 2, November 18, 2013.

58 See, for example, Muhtaseb, 2013.

59 ILO, 2012. Also see Migration Policy Center, 2013.

60 Interview 15, September 7, 2014.

61 ILO, 2012, p. 11.

62 See, for example, Integrated Regional Information Network, 2006; Olwan, 2007; and Abu Farhah, 2012.

have several NGOs.[63] But it is likely that unofficial nonnational workers meet the majority of employer demands for low-paid, low-skilled manual labor in Jordan. Chapters Three and Four of this report show how this dynamic directly bears on the role of Syrian refugees in Jordan.

Summary of Stability Issues as of Late 2014

Jordan is stable, but its current and near- to midterm stability is dependent on consistent and, likely, increasing support from the United States, other Western allies, and regional Gulf Arab states. Internal security services are competent, and they are able to manage the security situation in Amman, and in most of the north and far south as well. Ma'an remains a concern, but at least, as of late 2014, it did not appear to be generating any existential threats. Water is a pressing issue, but the Red to Dead project might help forestall catastrophe. Political and economic issues are of greater but not existential concern in the near- to midterm.

While most polls and reports segregate political, economic, and social concerns, in reality these are inextricably linked. Hirak-style activism among normally loyal East Bankers stems, in part, from concerns with corruption and government ineffectiveness, but also it also stems, in part, from mounting social and economic pressures. Lack of economic opportunity—or the perceived lack of opportunity—might not be the direct spark behind a prospective protest or revolt, but it might be a major contributing factor to emerging antigovernment sentiment. One interviewee stated, "Economic will turn into political will turn into incitement and into rifts."[64] Yet this same interviewee believed that the safest bet for the King and for the GoJ was to maintain the political, social, and economic status quo. In other words, the kingdom's stability depends on sustaining the historic yet delicate balance between all of the competing factors that continue to threaten Jordan. The following chapters describe how the Syrian refugees might affect efforts to bring Jordan back to an imagined "old normal," as well as how the refugees might help Jordan find a new state of normality that is mutually beneficial to all local, regional, and global parties of interest.

Perhaps the greatest stabilizing factor in Jordan is the constant, vivid reporting on the chaos and violence in Syria and Iraq, as well as on the social unrest across North Africa and the Arab Gulf. Sources cited in this report indicated that Jordanians who are unhappy with their government are also unwilling to risk throwing Jordan into chaos by seeking redress through violence or other destabilizing means. Positive, willing popular support for the government would be more sustainable and provide Jordan with greater resiliency in the face of unexpected internal crisis than this negative stability. However, negative stability has given Jordan time to cope with the aftermath of the Arab Spring, to address long-standing grievances, and to deal with the Syrian refugee crisis.

---

[63] See, for example, ILO, 2012.

[64] Interview 2, November 18, 2013.

CHAPTER THREE

Economic Factors and Forecasted Impact

This chapter describes the degree to which Syrians benefit from and affect Jordan's economy, describes other economic issues associated with Syrian refugees, and presents a forecast of Syrian refugee impacts on Jordan's economy and such economic stability factors as unemployment and consumer prices. Most Syrian refugees in Jordan live outside official camps and are at least partly integrated into local economies in primarily north and central Jordan. Many refugees are at least partly dependent on aid. It is not possible to determine how many of these refugees will ultimately attempt to settle in Jordan on a permanent basis, but their decision to attempt permanent settlement will hinge, at least in part, on economic opportunity. The degree to which Syrian refugee families—both those who will try to stay and those who plan to return to Syria—benefit from gainful employment will have many wide-ranging effects on the refugees and on Jordanian municipalities. These effects include, but are not limited to, (1) vulnerability to extremist or criminal recruiting, (2) continued dependence on aid, (3) social integration into host communities, (4) internal migration in Jordan or further displacement, and (5) the degree to which Syrian refugees contribute to or detract from Jordan's economy. All of these factors are closely linked with Jordan's continuing stability.

Current Economic Status and Economic Integration of Syrian Refugees

Data on Syrian refugee dependence on aid, formal employment, and informal or off-the-books employment in Jordan vary considerably and have changed since the first waves of refugees crossed the border in 2011. Several 2012 baseline studies showed that the majority of Syrian refugees were male, were married, and had less than a high school education.[1] As of 2014, the registered population of women exceeded men by a small margin. According to these UNHCR data, women made up a significant majority of refugees over the age of 18, and many households were led by women.[2] Because they need to spend so much time at home, women heading households with young children might find it difficult to work, although there have been concerted efforts to promote entrepreneurship among Syrian women.[3] NGO programs have focused on aid to female heads of household and on offering opportunities for female employment. Jordanian women have, in many cases, been particularly welcoming of Syrian

[1] See, for example, Olwan and Shiyab, 2012; and CARE, 2012.

[2] REACH, 2014a. The *Jordan Response Plan 2015 for the Syria Crisis* states that 23.5 percent of all Syrian refugees are women. Ministry of Planning and International Cooperation, 2014, p. 6.

[3] See, for example, MacBride, 2013; and UNDP, undated.

female refugees and have provided them with homes and business opportunities. Therefore, while these female-headed refugee households are considered part of an at-risk population, the women and their children pose less of an economic, social, and security risk than a prima facie analysis might imply.

Syrian refugee concerns about economic opportunity are pronounced. These concerns were well founded in 2012, when sample-driven studies showed that approximately three-fourths of refugees had a family income of less than 250 Jordanian dinars; this places them well below the official poverty level.[4] Some reports show that employment has improved since 2012, but one 2014 study showed that more than three-fourths of Syrians thought that there were insufficient employment opportunities, and more than three-fourths thought that challenges to their livelihoods were "very" or "extremely" urgent.[5] Data through 2012 and 2014 indicated that Syrians were incurring debt to keep their families afloat.[6] While debt-to-income ratios might have improved among some Syrian refugees since 2012, some of this improvement is because of seasonal labor opportunities in the agricultural sector.[7] Dependence on this kind of inconsistent, seasonal labor might do a great deal to keep Syrian refugee unemployment high and hidden in the informal economy, where it cannot be tracked or addressed by the GoJ or NGOs.

Of perhaps greater concern were the indications in focus groups, interviews, and polls that some Syrian men felt emasculated by their inability to find work or by having to depend on female members of their households for income.[8] Some of these frustrations might be channeled against their own family members, but there are also indications that lack of employment has made some Syrian males vulnerable to criminal recruitment or more liable to lash out in schools, at informal or temporary job locations, or on the streets.[9] While data on Syrian refugee violence is mostly anecdotal, there have been reports of fighting and low-level violence in the north of Jordan.[10] There is no empirical evidence indicating how many Syrian males have joined criminal gangs or been enlisted into extremist groups, so the security risks associated with refugee unemployment are mostly based on conjecture.[11]

Many Jordanians believe that Syrian refugees are snapping up all available jobs and are thereby reducing opportunities for young Jordanian men and women.[12] Jordanians "blame Syrian men for pricing their labor below the market rate. . . . Jordanian men see themselves

---

[4] The 2010 poverty line was 813.7 dinars in income, per individual, per year. See UNDP, 2013c, p. 34. Also see CARE, 2012; and Olwan and Shiyab, 2012. Also see the web page for the United Nations Millennium Development Goals Indicators for Jordan.

[5] REACH, 2014a, p. 1; also see UNHCR, 2013.

[6] See, for example, CARE, 2012; UNHCR, 2013; REACH 2014a; and Serrato, 2014.

[7] REACH, 2014c.

[8] See, for example, REACH 2014a.

[9] Leigh, 2014. The empirical value of the information in this article is unclear.

[10] UNHCR, 2014d, p. 14; Mercy Corps, 2012, pp. 5–6.

[11] There might be classified data that address this issue, but the magnitude of the problem and the limited access to extremist groups make it highly unlikely that these data would provide consistent or defensible quantitative bases for a holistic analysis of the impact of unemployment on recruitment.

[12] Mercy Corps, 2012; REACH, 2014a; CARE, 2012; Ajluni and Kawar, 2014; Dhingra, 2014.

passed over in favor of the cheaper option."[13] These perceptions exist in such areas of refugee concentration as Irbid, Mafraq, Zarqa, and less wealthy parts of Amman, and the belief that Syrians are "stealing" Jordanian jobs has become widespread.[14] There does not appear to be much empirical evidence to support this perception. Syrian laborers often take jobs in the informal market and, in many cases, perform functions that would normally be performed by nonnational or itinerant workers—for example, Egyptians or, prior to Syria's collapse in 2011, seasonal Syrian workers.[15] More important, unemployment rates do not show consistent increases even in high refugee concentration areas. A 2014 report showed that unemployment in Mafraq—a governorate with a particularly high density of Syrian refugees—actually declined by 1.1 percent between 2010 and 2013.[16] This same report concluded:

> Despite the rapid increase in Syrian refugee labour force activity in the four governorates [Mafraq, Irbid, Zarqa, and Amman], there is little change in the total number of economically active Jordanians there. . . . [T]he rate of increase of the unemployment rate in the country at large was greater than in the four governorates [with the highest refugee populations].[17]

These data are not sufficiently reliable to make an empirical argument that Jordanian unemployment fears are unfounded. One Jordanian businessman interviewed by RAND saw the direct impact of cheap Syrian labor on informal employment: "A Jordanian painter receives about 10 JD [Jordanian dinars] an hour, while a Syrian will take 4 JD per hour. They compete for manual labor, stores, taking our jobs."[18] However, after comparing all available data—and after reviews of Jordanian media, Jordanian Arabic YouTube content in late 2013 and early 2014, interviews, and survey results (cited herein)—with the reported unemployment data, it *appears* that the threat of Syrian workers "stealing" Jordanian jobs is generally exaggerated. But this does not make the perception of the threat any less real or any less meaningful when taking into consideration the willingness of Jordanian communities to continue to accept Syrian refugees' presence. In turn, the disparity between data and perception is irrelevant if many young Syrian males are made to feel unwanted in Jordan, are denied labor, and have no opportunity to emigrate or repatriate. So far the labor issue has not created major or irreparable rifts between Jordanians and Syrian refugees, but it is an issue that deserves close attention.

Finally, and perhaps most important for the issue of Jordanian stability, the Syrian refugees are placing a tremendous burden on Jordanian national, regional, and municipal budgets and service delivery. Because such a significant majority of Syrians live off camp, it is nearly impossible to determine the full scope of the impact of impoverished, underemployed, and dependent households on Jordanian services.[19] For many off-camp Syrians, conditions and job opportunities are improving, and these dependencies are a threat to the budget only if donor

---

[13] Mercy Corps, 2012, p. 4.

[14] Nearly all interviewees for this report described this trend, although most believed that it was overstated.

[15] Interview 2, November 18, 2013; interview 3, November 18, 2013; and interview 6, November 18, 2013, among others.

[16] Ajluni and Kawar, 2014, p. 19.

[17] Ajluni and Kawar, 2014, p. 18.

[18] Interview 13, February 2, 2014.

[19] Nearly all of the reports cited in this section refer in some way to these budget impacts.

support wavers or fails to meet any increases in demand. There are many legal ways to employ Syrians in Jordan; there are opportunities to purchase work visas, and Syrian companies also have access to the Jordanian market.[20] While it might be reasonable to assess dependent Syrian refugees as a drain on the budget and local services, for purposes of understanding threats to stability, it is more useful to assess the Syrian refugees in terms of national opportunity and in the context of long-standing symbiotic international relationships.

Jordan has been and continues to be the Middle East's regional "safety valve" for displaced persons.[21] In return for accepting and protecting millions of refugees since the mid-twentieth century, Jordan is compensated by donor states. The United States and Arab Gulf states recognize Jordan's vital role by sustaining and, from time to time, increasing direct and indirect support to the national budget and economy. While Jordanian officials complain about the stress that refugees place on their economy—many of these complaints are well founded—they also tend to see clear and needed financial value in the concomitant aid money. This dynamic is evident in *Jordan Response Plan 2015 for the Syria Crisis* (published in December 2014), a comprehensive strategy designed to address needs of all the Syrian refugees in Jordan and to improve both refugee and community resilience.[22] In this plan, the GoJ justifies requirements for approximately 2.87 billion U.S. dollars, the majority of which will likely have to be sourced from donors.[23]

Forecast: The Impact of Syrian Refugees on Jordan's Economic Stability

Barring the highly unlikely possibility of mass repatriation, Syrian refugees will continue to burden the Jordanian national budget and strain governorate and municipal service delivery in north and central Jordan.[24] However, absent a significant influx of *new* refugees, it appears that the situation has stabilized and that the GoJ has a good understanding of the challenges associated with caring for and providing employment to the displaced Syrians. The Azraq Camp in eastern Jordan provides a way for the GoJ to keep new refugees away from major population centers and away from the already-crowded and sometimes difficult-to-control Zaatari Camp. If donor support remains at current levels or increases to address the requirements in the *Jordan Response Plan 2015 for the Syria Crisis*, then the economic impact of Syrian refugees on Jordan

---

[20] The official GoJ English website has instructions and fees for obtaining work visas and work permits. However, there was insufficient objective evidence to describe how easy or difficult it is for Syrian refugees—documented and undocumented—to obtain a valid work permit, as of late 2014.

[21] This concept emerged in many of the literature references cited in this report and was reinforced during interviews. In particular, interviewees 17 and 18, November 23, 2014, pressed home the idea of the regional "safety valve" and stressed that this was a positive local and regional dynamic.

[22] Ministry of Planning and International Cooperation, 2014.

[23] Ministry of Planning and International Cooperation, 2014, p. 10. The table on this page provides estimates of impacts and costs.

[24] This forecast represents the informed expert analysis of the principal investigator and is derived from the literature, video, interviews, survey data, and discussions cited herein. It relies most heavily on the meta-analysis of the finished survey reports and the interview responses. All expert analytic forecasting, whether it is singular or part of a collective process, requires conjecture. All forecasts should be considered starting points for, or inputs to, additional analyses. All forecasts should be read with the understanding that the future is inherently unpredictable. Terms of estimative probability are used where appropriate (see Kent, 1964). These caveats also apply to the forecasts in the following chapters of the report.

is unlikely to worsen. Syrians will continue to absorb many of the low-paying, low-skill jobs within Jordan's informal economy, and more Syrians are likely to migrate south and southwest to Salt, Karak, Tafileh, and Aqaba. But current laws will prevent most Syrians from affecting the formal economy or higher-end blue- and white-collar employment.[25]

Lack of employment, underemployment, and poverty will likely continue to leave large portions of the Syrian refugee population somewhat vulnerable to criminal and extremist recruitment. This issue is addressed further in Chapter Five. However, it is *unlikely* that significant portions of the Syrian refugee population will be enticed to join illicit or terrorist organizations solely because they lack sufficient employment. Aid delivery is improving in many areas, and the various NGO efforts across north and central Jordan will continue to provide an economic safety net. There will continue to be sufficient opportunities in the informal economy to help counterbalance other options. That said, it is almost certain that *some* Syrian refugees will conduct criminal activity, primarily because they lack other options, and economic factors might play into the decision of other refugees to participate in extremist activity. It will remain difficult to determine the scale of this threat and the degree to which these actions will be motivated by lack of economic opportunity. These questions will almost certainly continue to present difficult analytic challenges.

Syrian refugees are also likely to benefit the Jordanian economy in several ways. Most obviously, the sheer scale of the refugee problem has given the GoJ a reasonable basis for requesting sizable and continuing donor support. As demonstrated in donor investments from 2012 to 2014, and as estimated in the *Jordan Response Plan 2015 for the Syria Crisis*, this support is likely to benefit not only the Syrian refugees but also most Jordanians and existing refugees from other nations. While this money is rightly intended to support and sustain the Syrian refugees, if it is sufficiently funded, this plan will have many ancillary benefits, including the development of infrastructure across central and northern Jordan, significant improvements in government service delivery capabilities, improvements to municipal budgets and capabilities, and reduction in chronic unemployment among Syrian refugees *and* Jordanian nationals. More important, it will help guarantee the financial stability of the GoJ through 2015 and will possibly strengthen ties between Jordan, its partners in the Gulf, and the United States and other Western allies: The financial crisis spurred by the Syrian refugees has already highlighted Jordan's strategic value to many high-level officials in the United States.

Because many Syrian refugees are entrepreneurial and already have useful manual or technical skills, over time it seems likely that many will improve rather than burden Jordan's economy.[26] These benefits might or might not bear fruit in 2015, but barring stringent efforts to prevent Syrians from seeking employment in Jordan, they are likely to have an overall positive impact for small businesses, the agricultural sector, and municipal development. As more Syrian men and women are gainfully employed, and as more are able to start small businesses, they will place less stress on municipal services and be likelier to contribute to other local businesses as they increase spending on goods and services. Legal limits on Syrian refugee employment might inhibit this process, but these limits might also prevent an overheating of the economy in such places as Irbid and Mafraq. The balance between underemployment and

[25] Technically, Syrian refugees cannot be employed in Jordan without a permit, and these permits are very difficult to obtain. Most Syrians who are employed are employed in the informal economy without permits and, more than likely, without paying taxes or obtaining licenses, when those are necessary.

[26] See, e.g., Alafi and Alfawaeer, 2014.

overheating local economies will be difficult to maintain, and Syrian employment will continue to be difficult to understand and manage for many years.

Perceptions of the Syrian refugees' impact on employment are unlikely to change in the near term, and these perceptions might worsen as Syrians become more adept at finding work. However, further empirical studies of the true impact of Syrian refugees on employment will likely start to find a footing in Jordanian local media. If data through 2015 continue to bear out the findings in the 2014 ILO report by Ajluni and Kawar, then Jordanian officials can start to counter the prevailing wisdom that Syrians are "stealing" Jordanian jobs. However, championing Syrian refugee employment will be problematic for several reasons. First, it would officially acknowledge and perhaps encourage the violation of Jordanian laws against unapproved refugee employment. Second, it would be unpopular in the largest Jordanian municipalities and therefore politically risky. And, third, it might indicate that the GoJ is laying the groundwork for the eventual incorporation of Syrian refugees as Jordanian citizens. While integration is ultimately possible, it is not currently GoJ policy, and (based on anecdotal reports cited herein) it is a generally unpopular concept. The issue of integration is addressed in Chapter Four.

CHAPTER FOUR

Social Factors and Forecasted Impact

This chapter describes the degree to which off-camp Syrian refugees have been integrated into Jordanian communities, social issues associated with the refugee camps, and other evolving social issues. It also forecasts the impact of Syrian refugees on Jordan's social and political stability. Even though this report is divided into functional categories—economic, social, and security—in practice, there are no clear divisions: Economic hardships and perceptions strongly affect social dynamics, and, in turn, both positive and negative social interactions appear to affect Jordanians' willingness to accept Syrians into the informal and formal economy. All of these issues affect and are affected by security concerns. Nonetheless, there are some distinct and empirical findings regarding social issues that are relevant to assessments of stability.

Assessing Late-2014 Social Integration and Social Impacts of Syrian Refugees

Jordanians' perceptions of Syrian refugees are somewhat bifurcated between the in-camp and off-camp refugee populations, though economic factors and stresses on municipal service delivery tend to dominate overall perceptions. The first studies of Jordanians' perceptions of Syrian refugees emerged in 2012. These revealed a complex Jordanian response to Syrian refugees.[1] For the most part, Jordanians along the Syrian border openly welcomed Syrians into their homes and their communities. There were many reported cases of Jordanian families accepting Syrians they did not know into their homes, while in other cases there were cross-border familial or tribal relationships that influenced willingness to accept refugee families.[2] Yet immediate tensions emerged. Many Jordanians quickly assessed that the Syrians were taking their jobs, though the mostly unemployed Syrian men were equally frustrated that they could not find meaningful employment.[3] Friction between Syrian and Jordanian teenagers, both in and out of school, led to a general sense of unease in some parts of northern Jordan.[4] Over time, Jordanians in the north became increasingly frustrated that Syrians were straining municipal services, and it appears that these frustrations carried over into a broader national sentiment.[5]

1 For example, see Mercy Corps 2012; CARE, 2012; Olwan and Shiyab, 2012; and UNDP, 2013d.

2 Interview 6, November 18, 2013; see, e.g., UNHCR, 2013.

3 Mercy Corps, 2012; CARE, 2012; Olwan and Shiyab, 2012.

4 Most surveys showed that, between 2012 and 2014, approximately 60 percent of Syrian children did not attend school.

5 This assessment is based on the analysis of all cited reference material. These sentiments emerged in both anecdotal quotes and empirical surveys.

Many Syrians are also frustrated and believe that they are not welcome in Jordan, but this sentiment is far from overwhelming. Anecdotal reports and interviews highlighted some very real concerns about social tensions and perceived animosities, but one study showed that most Syrians have better perceptions of their integration than Jordanians do. A robust early 2014 study by REACH showed a side-by-side comparison between Jordanian and Syrian perceptions on issues ranging from service delivery to social tensions.[6] In general, Syrians were more positive about government services, less concerned about social tensions, and more optimistic about employment opportunities. But the most-remarkable result showed that while only 34 percent of Jordanians had a positive or very positive view of Syrian refugees, 77 percent of Syrians had a positive view of Jordanians.[7] On the one hand, this result somewhat helps to alleviate concerns that Syrian refugees present a serious threat to Jordanians; the refugees are not, as a group, inclined to undermine their hosts, and they generally feel comfortable in Jordan.

On the other hand, the strong indications that many Jordanians are frustrated with and actively dislike Syrians—39 percent of Jordanians had a negative or very negative view of Syrians in the REACH study—is cause for concern.[8] A three-year longitudinal survey, by the University of Jordan's Center for Strategic Studies, on Jordanian perceptions showed steadily increasing support for Bashar Al-Assad's regime in Syria, steadily decreasing support for the mostly Sunni opposition, decreasing interest in the subject of Syria, and steadily increasing reluctance to accept more Syrian refugees.[9] The Center for Strategic Studies study showed that, in September 2011, 64 percent of Jordanians rejected the idea of accepting more Syrian refugees, while in August 2014, that number jumped to 79 percent of national respondents.[10] Therefore, it appears that Jordanians are frustrated with the Syria crisis in general and specifically with Syrian refugees.

On the surface, this trend does not bode well for the GoJ's efforts to support the hundreds of thousands of Syrian refugees living in host communities. If social tensions continue to mount, then Jordanians' resentment of Syrians might reverse the positive trends in Syrians' perceptions of Jordanians. This, in turn, could undermine security and stability in Jordan. *However*, thus far the positive trends in Syrians' perception have not been reversed. Based on a meta-assessment of all of the studies cited in this report, it appears instead that Syrians' perceptions of Jordanians, of their lives in Jordan, and of their social inclusion are either holding steady or improving. There have been some incidents of violence or social friction between Jordanians and Syrians, but these have been quite few in number considering the sizable contingent of refugees integrated into densely packed municipalities, such as Irbid and Mafraq. As of late 2014, it appeared that Jordanians resent but generally accept Syrians living among them on a day-to-day basis. One Jordanian businessman who resented the impact of inexpen-

---

6 This study comprised 1,445 interviews across 446 separate communities in north and central Jordan. REACH, 2014a, p. 7.

7 REACH, 2014a, p. 26.

8 REACH, 2014a, p. 26. Other studies also indicated Jordanian frustration with Syrians, but I did not find another study that was immediately comparable to the results from the REACH report.

9 Al Khatib, 2014, pp. 17–19. Direct comparisons to these data are difficult to find, but in a 2012 poll by the Arab Center for Research and Policy Studies, 82 percent of respondents supported regime change in Syria, while in the 2014 Center for Strategic Studies study, only 35 percent of national respondents supported the opposition in Syria. Arab Center for Research and Policy Studies, 2012, p. 4; Al Khatib, 2014, p. 17.

10 Al Khatib, 2014, p. 19.

sive Syrian labor on employment opportunities stated: "They work for little money, but I don't know if they'll cause . . . troubles. Most people who came are frightened average citizens."[11] There appears to be some distance between Jordanians' overarching negative sentiment and their more neutral or positive behavior.

Forecast: Impact of Syrian Refugees on Jordan's Social Stability

Ongoing social tension between Jordanians and Syrians is inevitable, but as of late 2014, there were no strong indicators that Jordanians' anti-Syrian sentiment will result in social unrest or destabilizing violence.[12] Despite their misgivings, Jordanians are becoming accustomed to, or perhaps resigned to, the presence of this latest wave of Syrian refugees. If the national polls fail to translate into actual social friction, then the GoJ can leverage funding for the 2015 response plan to alleviate Jordanian-Syrian tensions and, ultimately, reduce social threats to national stability.[13] The greater social threat to Jordanian stability is the degree to which Jordanians perceive the GoJ successfully handles or, conversely, mishandles the refugee crisis.

Jordanians, and particularly East Bankers, are becoming more socially and politically aware and active.[14] Nearly all data on Jordanians' perceptions emphasize social and political concerns above economic and security concerns. All of the specific concerns about the impact and handling of Syrian refugee issues contribute to a broader sense of unease among Jordanians, both in the most-affected areas in the north and, notably, in parts of Amman that have less Syrian presence. Throughout 2015, Jordanians are likely to continue to assess their situation in the context of the chaos in Syria, Iraq, and North Africa, but their expectations for government performance are likely to continue to increase. There will be considerable pressure on the GoJ to capitalize on the 2015 response plan.

Jordanians will expect the government to address the pressure points identified in local and national surveys (primarily municipal services, infrastructure, and employment), but also in the plan itself. By stating in the plan that the GoJ intends to improve nearly all aspects of Jordanian life to help support the Syrian refugees, it has set an expectation for performance.[15] The amount of money dedicated to improvements will be made widely known, both in print and through other formal and informal media. If services, infrastructure, and employment do not visibly improve over the course of 2015, most Jordanians will become increasingly frustrated with both the GoJ and the Syrian refugees. Social stability does not hinge entirely on the successful application of the 2015 response plan, but it is likely that Jordanians will view government performance vis-à-vis the plan as a critical metric. Some 2014 data show that the GoJ and its partners have significant room to improve performance.[16]

---

[11] Interview 13, February 2, 2014.

[12] The forecasting caveats from Chapter Three apply to this chapter.

[13] Ministry of Planning and International Cooperation, 2014.

[14] This is an informed subjective assessment based on examinations of Jordanian history and periodic direct observation of Jordan between 2002 and 2014.

[15] These expectations are set throughout the summary and also in the details of the draft December 1, 2014 version of the plan cited in the bibliography.

[16] See, for example, REACH, 2014b. This study showed that support to off-camp Syrian refugees was less than adequate in early 2014.

It is highly likely that there will be limited social unrest attributable to Syrian refugees throughout 2015. Some of this is likely to emerge in such cities as Salt, Karak, and Tafileh, where refugee populations are smaller than in the north but unemployment is (or is perceived to be) a significant economic and social problem. No protest or social disturbance will have an identifiable unitary cause, so it will be difficult for analysts to attribute incidents to social friction caused by the presence of Syrian refugees; analysts should be cautious not to accept interpretations of incidents at face value. It is possible, but not likely, that there will be significant social unrest on the part of either off-camp or in-camp Syrian refugees. It appears that most know they are in a vulnerable position in Jordan, and that despite their continuing poverty and underemployment, they will have a better immediate future in Jordan than in Syria.[17] *Negative stability* will influence Syrians' perceptions and behavior just as it influences Jordanians' perceptions and behavior.

---

[17] In some cases, this also means that Syrians are reluctant to confront Jordanians on issues of social welfare, law and order, or interpersonal disputes over wages or similar issues. Data from a 2014 Oxfam study showed that many Syrian men felt that they would not be treated fairly if brought before a Jordanian court. Serrato, 2014, p. 26.

CHAPTER FIVE

Security Assessment and Forecasted Impact

This chapter briefly assesses the late-2014 impact of Syrian refugees on Jordan's internal security and then assesses impacts through 2015. The security assessment and forecast are limited in scope because a sizable portion of the most relevant and timely security data is classified by either the GoJ or the U.S. government. This assessment should be used to contribute to, or to help outline, classified assessments. However, the importance of classified security information for the assessing and forecasting of Jordan's stability should not be overstated. Long-term open-source analyses cannot pinpoint specific threats or reveal the most-immediate intentions of threat groups, but these analyses are often more useful for broader trend analysis and forecasting because they are not overly focused on near-term reporting.

Impact of Syrian Refugees on Jordanian Security as of Late 2014

As of late 2014, there did not appear to be any public reports of significant security threat *trends* to the GoJ from the Syrian refugee community. While classified reporting might or might not indicate threats, there is no empirical data showing that Syrian refugees, *as a group*, present an explicit security threat to the GoJ, to the King, or to Jordan's stability. There have been several small-scale riots in Zaatari Camp, and there have been individual security incidents reported in Irbid, Mafraq, Zarqa, and Amman since 2011.[1] However, the publicly reported off-camp incidents—ostensibly more dangerous than in-camp incidents because they cannot be as closely observed and controlled—do not appear to exceed normal incident reporting for Jordan.[2] Jordanian nationals joining extremist groups in Syria might present more of a threat to Jordan's stability than Syrians joining extremist or criminal groups in Jordan.[3] There are unclassified reports of cross-border criminal gang activity in northern Jordan, and official statistics show that all reported criminal activity in northern Jordan rose between 2011 and

[1] See, for example, U.S. Department of State, 2013; and U.S. Department of State, 2014.

[2] This assessment is based on a review of English-language reporting in *The Jordan Times*, primarily, and in online journals between late 2013 and late 2014, as well as the Jordan crime and safety report summaries from the U.S. Department of State. Even this assessment shows that incidents related to Syrian refugees might be *overstated* because of the media and social sensitivities associated with the refugee population. *This is an informed subjective assessment based on an informal survey of data from English-only sources.* A definitive finding would require the acquisition of all incident reporting from the GoJ, possibly dating back to 2007, to provide a sufficient baseline of data and a longitudinal analysis from early 2011 (the start of the Arab Spring and the refugee influx) through late 2014.

[3] See, for example, Ma'ayeh, 2013.

2013.[4] GoJ efforts to redirect new refugees to the isolated Azraq Camp were intended to alleviate some of this activity.[5]

This is not to say that all Syrians are nonviolent. There have been reports of Syrian refugees joining criminal gangs in Jordan. Some portions of the teenage and adult male populations are almost certainly involved in or directly support the antiregime militias in Syria. Others might be affiliated with such groups as Al-Nusra Front or the Islamic State. However, because the Jordanian security services generally excel at identifying internal threats, and because the many nonviolent Syrian refugees fear being expelled from Jordan if affiliated with terrorism, there is considerable incentive for extremists within the Syrian refugee community to remain inconspicuous. Based on the dearth of unclassified reporting of serious incidents between 2011 and 2014, any extremists in the refugee community have been suppressed, expelled, or have chosen to remain mostly inactive. In all likelihood, they use Jordan as an area to rest, recuperate, and conduct planning and logistics for action in Syria and (possibly) Iraq, rather than within Jordan. While it would be ideal to completely eliminate the threat of violent extremism from the Syrian refugee population, the absence of a large-scale threat to security and stability is also desirable.[6]

Serious threats *against* Syrians are few and far between. Most Syrians believe that they are safe in Jordan and, barring some reports of threats at work, they are generally willing to accept protection from the GoJ and from their host communities. One 2014 study reported that approximately 80 percent of in-camp refugees felt safe, while 87 percent of off-camp refugees felt safe. Nearly 50 percent of off-camp refugees stated that they would seek help from the police if they had a security problem.[7] This is a remarkably high percentage, considering the degree to which most Syrian refugees were alienated from government security services throughout their lives in Syria. In 2013, researchers from Georgetown University summarized security-related findings from their broader study: "Refugees from Syria reported feeling extremely safe and secure in Jordan, and in our interviews repeatedly expressed their gratitude to the government and people for hosting them."[8] Although it is not universally shared, this general sense of security in the Syrian refugee community through at least late 2014 likely contributes to the unwillingness of most Syrians to engage in high-profile criminal or extremist activity.

Forecast: The Impact of Syrian Refugees on Jordan's Security

There will almost certainly be security incidents involving Syrian refugees throughout 2015 and beyond.[9] Any population of more than 600,000 people will necessarily include some

---

[4] Department of Statistics, 2013b, p. 2. For example, reported crimes in Mafraq rose from 1,751 in 2011 to 2,146 in 2013, an increase of approximately 23 percent. Also see Sale, 2013; Al Sharif, 2013; U.S. Department of State, 2013, 2014; and Kimmelman, 2014.

[5] See, for example, "Syrian Refugees in Jordan: Carefully Watched," 2014.

[6] Determining the existence and scope of such a threat would require reference to classified sources.

[7] Serrato, 2014, p. 5.

[8] Davis and Taylor, 2013, p. 11. On the same page, they also state that dark-skinned refugees reported more security incidents and greater fear of Jordanians than light-skinned refugees.

[9] The forecasting caveats from Chapter Three also apply to this chapter.

violent criminals, and because of the chaotic political situation in and around Jordan, some of those inclined to violence may also be inclined to join or support such extremist groups as Al-Nusra Front or the Islamic State. Poverty, exposure to extreme violence in Syria, and social frustrations might at some point lead to spikes in criminal activity across the broader Syrian refugee community. It is possible that Syrians might be involved with or lead a serious terrorist attack against Western or GoJ targets in Jordan. The way in which the GoJ and, to a lesser extent, the United States react to such incidents will shape the way they affect Jordanian stability. While it would be unwise to downplay the threat of extremist violence, failure to temper reactions to any incident related to the Syrian refugee population is likely to contribute to anti-Syrian sentiment in Jordan and anti-Jordanian sentiment among Syrian refugees. Both of these reactions would, in turn, be likely to undermine GoJ efforts to implement the ongoing refugee response plan.

Any erosion in security in the coming years—stemming from Syrian refugees, Jordanians, or others—will affect the ability of NGOs and municipalities to deliver critical services to refugees. A complex web of nearly 30 NGOs provide aid in cooperation with the United Nations programs in Jordan. These range from large-scale efforts at Zaatari in the north to smaller-scale projects and programs in smaller cities and towns, including Ma'an and Aqaba.[10] Because most NGOs are not able to fund or provide for their own security, they are prone to postpone or withdraw from projects when security degrades. Reduction in services would, in turn, feed some of the likely contributing factors to criminal activity, including unemployment and lack of health care, education, water, and shelter. If security incidents increase, further data collection and analysis should be conducted regarding the impact of security degradation on NGO service delivery.

[10] UNHCR, undated.

CHAPTER SIX

Conclusion, Summary Forecast, and Black Swan Warnings

Jordan was stable in late 2014. Despite the near-complete chaos in southern Syria and western Iraq, the Jordanian military has ably secured the borders from any sizable encroachment. The economy is vulnerable to major crises, but key allies have stepped in to help ensure that the GoJ can continue to fund itself and facilitate mostly adequate service delivery. Social pressures that built up during the past decade seem to have temporarily ebbed along with the Hirak movement, and so far the relationship between Jordanians and Syrian refugees has not led to widespread social unrest or bloodshed. Markers of ongoing concern, though, are evident across all sectors of Jordanian society. Shifting East Banker sentiment seems to be setting the stage for renewed rounds of protests. It remains to be seen how the arrest of the Jordanian Muslim Brotherhood leader in December 2014 will affect the attitudes of the rank and file of Jordan's "loyal opposition." Security issues persist despite the military's moves to the north: While Jordan's borders are secure, the situation in Ma'an remains unclear. Finally, while the water shortage does not present an imminent threat to service delivery, it does represent another long-term threat to stability that does not yet have a definitive solution.

Even though Jordan is not a major oil producer, it has still been vulnerable in recent decades to shifts in oil prices.[1] Oil prices dropped precipitously in late 2014. As of mid-December 2014, the price of oil was approximately 40 percent of the mid-2014 price.[2] This is actually positive in certain ways for Jordan and for the Jordanian response to the Syrian refugee crisis. The 2003–2011 war in Iraq and the Arab Spring protests in Egypt had left Jordan without its once-dependable supplies of cheap gasoline and natural gas. The resulting higher import prices were a heavy strain on the GoJ budget, so lower prices are likely to alleviate some of this pressure. Yet the uncertainty in oil-price trends will make it difficult for the GoJ to determine a viable subsidy plan.[3] Further, decreasing oil prices will decrease revenue for government donors in the Arab Gulf. While these donors are likely to continue to support Jordan, they are also likely to look to their own budget concerns before funneling hundreds of millions of dollars to a foreign government. At the very least, oil prices will continue to add an element of uncertainty into the Syrian refugee response.

Looking forward, it appears that Jordan is likely to continue on its present course. Barring one of a number of unlikely or unforeseen events, there is little chance that the Syrian refugee crisis will destabilize the government or unseat the Hashemite monarch. Instead, it appears likely that Jordan will face difficulties in 2015, and even continuing through 2016, with a series

[1] Mohaddes and Raissi, 2011.

[2] Udland, 2014.

[3] Obeidat, 2014c.

of economic, social, and security issues. But these issues are not likely to develop into crises. While the 2015 Syrian refugee response plan is logical and smartly designed to benefit both Syrians and Jordanians, its implementation will necessarily be imperfect and in all likelihood some funding will be uneven or untimely. Official unemployment figures are likely to decline during 2015, but the nature of the informal economy suggests that visible successes might be least relevant to the poorest Jordanians and Syrians. Some underlying conditions for instability will persist.

Jordan's continuing stability is dependent on the consistent and (likely) increasing support from the United States, other Western allies, and regional Gulf Arab states. Jordan has historically depended on a casual symbiotic relationship with a close ally—first with Great Britain during the Transjordan period and now with the United States.[4] These relationships appear to be either openly or grudgingly accepted by most Jordanians, as long as the relationships help the King and the government prevent Jordan from descending into the kind of chaos witnessed to the north and the east. King Abdullah II has moved ever closer to the United States and the West, and in the past year, he has taken up the challenges presented by the Syrian civil war and Iraqi unrest. The Syrian refugee crisis has given the King and the government leverage to make firm statements and firm decisions, most of which are directly aligned with the anti–Islamic State coalition. Refugee relief commitments by Western and Gulf allies demonstrate the kind of reciprocity likely to guarantee continued Jordanian support. The cornerstone of Jordanian internal stability is Jordan's close and continuing relationships with its external allies.

There are many analytic issues that must be addressed to ensure that decisionmakers are not caught off guard by emerging Syrian refugee trends or crises in the next few years. Through 2014, much attention was paid to the Zaatari Camp. This is unsurprising: The camp provided a microcosm of the Syrian refugee situation, it was accessible to aid workers and analysts, and refugees in the camp were more than willing to provide interesting anecdotes and to subject themselves to studies that might in turn reward them with improved services. There have been some excellent assessments of off-camp refugees, including a range of reports issued in 2015 after RAND's research for this report had concluded. Yet more analysts, in and out of government, would be well served by closer assessment of off-camp Syrian refugees. Issues with the off-camp population will determine whether, and then how, some portion of the 2011–2015 Syrian diaspora is integrated into Jordan's population. Instability in Ma'an and the large Syrian refugee populations in Irbid and Mafraq attract a great deal of attention, but the unease in Karak, Tafileh, and Salt should be paid greater attention. These midsize cities might be the proving grounds for Jordanian reform and for improvements in service delivery stemming from the 2015 refugee response funds. Finally, close attention should be paid to the way in which Jordanian and Western media respond to refugee-related incidents linked to violence or negative economic impacts. We can expect that the *reactions* to refugee-related incidents will be more important for stability than the incidents themselves.

Forecasting is inherently uncertain. The forecasts in report represent the probable or most-likely courses of events based on available evidence. The next section assesses black swan events, which seem less likely but carry a greater chance of undermining Jordan's stability.

---

[4] Abu Nowar, 2006; interviews 17 and 18, 2014.

Black Swans

This section assesses several black swan events that might undermine Jordan's stability. The term *black swan*, made popular by Nassim N. Taleb, has now entered into the analytic vernacular and is meant to describe highly improbable yet intensely dangerous or positive events.[5] Table 6.1 lists a series of improbable but possible events in the far left column, offers an estimate of possibility in the center column, and then describes the possible impacts of each event in the far right column. This list was developed during the literature review, interviews, and meta-analysis of survey data. A full list of events that might affect Jordanian stability would be far more extensive. This list focuses only on issues associated with the Syrian refugee population.

Table 6.1
Black Swan Events

Event	Possibility	Forecast Impact
The Islamic State seizes Dara'a, the city closest to Jordan's northern border	Possible but unlikely in early 2015	This would be expected to cause a massive influx of Syrian refugees into the border region with Jordan and an immediate humanitarian crisis, requiring extensive external support.
The Syrian regime collapses or is defeated by Sunni extremist groups	Highly unlikely through early 2015; unlikely after mid-2015	Depending on the nature of the collapse, this could result in gradual or even rapid repatriation of some Syrians in Jordan, as civilians seek to reclaim their homes, or it could lead to the increased displacement of Syrians into Jordan. This would be expected to also cause some social unrest in existing refugee populations.
The Islamic State or Al-Nusra Front claim control of Ma'an, Jordan	Highly unlikely at any time	This kind of extreme action, even if supported by most citizens in Ma'an, would not be expected to spread beyond Ma'an. It would almost certainly result in a severe military response by the GoJ.
The price of oil rebounds, rises above $140 per barrel, and stays there	Unlikely through 2015	At this price, continued U.S. support to Jordan would be difficult, although Arab Gulf countries would be expected to be far better positioned to provide support. The GoJ budget would likely be severely affected, as would many refugee response efforts. The Syrian economy would be expected to improve, and even with instability, some refugees might repatriate.
The price of oil drops below $30 per barrel and stays there	A lasting drop to this level is highly unlikely	At this price, continued Arab Gulf support to Jordan would likely be difficult, but the United States and Western allies could offer additional support. The GoJ budget and refugee response efforts would likely benefit overall.
A major terrorist attack by a Syrian refugee–led group against a GoJ target, resulting in a mass-casualty event	Unlikely	An immediate backlash against Syrian refugees would be expected to be all but inevitable. Both average Jordanians and the GoJ would likely work to isolate Syrians. Because Syrians are already well integrated into Jordanian society, this would be expected to lead to immediate friction and even social unrest if not checked.
The United States and Western allies withdraw support from Jordan	Highly unlikely	We can expect that this would be catastrophic and lead to immediate and considerable instability. Cross-border threat groups, including the Islamic State, might be emboldened to attack Jordan.
A peace deal in Syria that leads to stability and reconstruction	Highly unlikely through at least 2016, and even beyond	A significant portion of the Syrian refugee population in Jordan would likely repatriate, although possibly hundreds of thousands would be expected to decide to stay and integrate into Jordanian society or remain in the camps.

[5] Taleb, 2007.

Abbreviations

GDP	gross domestic product
GoJ	government of Jordan
ILO	International Labour Organization
JAF	Jordanian Armed Forces
NGO	nongovernmental organization
SME	subject-matter expert
UNDP	United Nations Development Programme
UNHCR	United Nations High Commissioner for Refugees
USAID	U.S. Agency for International Development

Bibliography

This section contains selected reference material. RAND analysts working on this project read and referred to thousands of media and social media sources to develop the findings herein. References selected here were specifically cited in the document or were used to inform the research findings and forecasts. All references cited and not cited in the document are included to provide additional resources for the sponsor and other analysts.

"700 Syrians Enter Jordan on Wednesday," *The Jordan Times*, December 4, 2013. As of January 28, 2015: http://jordantimes.com/700-syrians-enter-jordan-on-wednesday

"98,000 Guest Laborers Have Invalid Work Permits," *The Jordan Times*, November 3, 2013.

Abu Farha, Saba, "Illegal Egypt-Jordan Labor Permits' Trade Continues," Arab Reporters for Investigative Journalism, March 19, 2012.

Abumelhim, Mohammad Husni, "Women and Social Change in Jordanian Bedouin Society," *Studies in Sociology of Science*, Vol. 4, No. 4, 2013, pp. 27–31.

Abu Nowar, Maan, *The Development of Trans-Jordan 1929–1939: A History of the Hashemite Kingdom of Jordan*, Reading, UK: Ithaca Press, 2006.

Abuqudairi, Areej, "Anger Boils Over in the 'Fallujah of Jordan,'" *Al-Jazeera*, July 5, 2014. As of January 27, 2015:
http://www.aljazeera.com/news/middleeast/2014/07/anger-boils-over-fallujah-jordan-20147575130478577.html

"Activists Hold Sit-in for Prisoners in Israel," *The Jordan Times*, November 17, 2013. As of January 28, 2015: http://jordantimes.com/activists-hold-sit-in-for-prisoners-in-israel

Agence France-Presse, "Saudi Jails Jordanian Convicted of Spying for Israel," *YNet News*, October 30, 2013a. As of January 27, 2015:
http://www.ynetnews.com/articles/0,7340,L-4447610,00.html

———, "MERS Virus Strikes Jordanian Couple in UAE," *The Jordan Times*, November 30, 2013b. As of January 27, 2015:
http://jordantimes.com/mers-virus-strikes-jordanian-couple-in-uae

———, "Gun Prices, Sales Up in Jordan over Syria War Fears," Ma'an News Agency, January 17, 2014. As of January 27, 2015:
http://www.maannews.net/eng/ViewDetails.aspx?ID=665372

Ajluni, Salem, and Mary Kawar, *The Impact of the Syrian Refugee Crisis on the Labour Market in Jordan: A Preliminary Analysis*, Beirut: International Labour Organization Regional Office for Arab States, 2014. As of January 27, 2015:
http://www.ilo.org/wcmsp5/groups/public/---arabstates/---ro-beirut/documents/publication/wcms_242021.pdf

Akin, David, "Canada Gives $105 Million More to Jordan for Help with Syrian Crisis," *Toronto Sun*, January 23, 2014. As of January 27, 2015:
http://www.torontosun.com/2014/01/23/canada-gives-105-million-more-to-jordan-for-help-with-syrian-crisis

Alafi, Khaled K., and Moayyad Alfawaeer, "Syrians and Business in Irbid City: Jordanian Stability and Refugees: A Qualitative Study," *International Journal of Business and Management*, Vol. 9, No. 6, 2014, pp. 115–125.

Al-Ansari, Nadhir, N. Alibrahiem, M. Alsaman, and Sven Knutsson, "Water Demand Management in Jordan," *Engineering*, Vol. 6, No. 1, 2014, pp. 19–26.

Al-Ansari, Nadhir, Salem Al-Oun, Wafa Hadad, and Sven Knutsson, "Water Loss in Mafraq Governorate, Jordan," *Natural Science*, Vol. 5, No. 3, 2013, pp. 333–340.

Al-Daameh, Mohamed, "Misunderstood Ma'an," *Asharq Al-Awsat*, July 16, 2014. As of January 27, 2015: http://www.aawsat.net/2014/07/article55334318

Al Emam, Dana, "Education System in Need of Complete Overhaul—Academics," *The Jordan Times*, December 3, 2013. As of May 15, 2015: http://http://www.jordantimes.com/news/local/education-system-need-complete-overhaul-%E2%80%94-academics

Al Hayat Center, "A Study Investigating the Trends Within the Jordanian Society Regarding Political Parties, Political Knowledge, and Participation in the Elections," Researches and Studies Unit, Amman, Jordan, 2012.

Al Khatib, Walid, *Public Opinion Poll: Some Current National and Regional Issues*, Amman, Jordan: Center for Strategic Studies, University of Jordan, September 2014. As of January 27, 2015: http://css.ju.edu.jo/Photos/635478411873156800.pdf

Al-Omari, A., A. Salman, and E. Karablieh, "The Red Dead Canal Project: An Adaptation Option to Climate Change in Jordan," *Desalination and Water Treatment*, Vol. 52, No. 13, 2013, pp. 2833–2840.

Alqadi, Khaled A., and Lalit Kumar, "Water Policy in Jordan," *International Journal of Water Resources Development*, Vol. 30, No. 2, 2014, pp. 322–334.

"Al Rai, JT Employees Decide to Observe One-Day Strike," *The Jordan Times*, November 10, 2013. As of January 28, 2015: http://jordantimes.com/jpf-employees-reject-appointment-of-new-board-members-to-continue-protests

"Al Rai Workers Demand Apology for Gendarmerie Storming Paper's Offices," *The Jordan Times*, November 6, 2013. As of January 28, 2015: http://jordantimes.com/al-rai-workers-demand-apology-for-gendarmerie-storming-papers-offices

Al-Rawashdah, "Kuwaiti Grant to Fund Major Development Projects in Jordan," *Al-Shorfa*, October 13, 2012a.

———, "Saudi Arabia Grants Jordan $787 Million to Finance Development Projects," *Al-Shorfa*, December 4, 2012b.

———, "Jordan Confronts al-Qaeda Schemes Inside and Outside the Kingdom," *Al Shorfa*, November 6, 2013.

Al-Saraireh, Shadi Irshaid, "The Relationship Between Unemployment Rate in Jordan with Rates of Foreign Labor Force, Government Expenditure, and Economic Growth," *International Journal of Business and Social Science*, Vol. 3, No. 3, March 2014, pp. 294–301.

Al Sharif, Osama, "Jordan's Daraa Problem," *Al-Monitor*, December 8, 2013. As of January 27, 2015: http://www.al-monitor.com/pulse/originals/2013/12/jordan-daraa-salafist-jihad.html#

Althbutat, Qasem, and Nermin Ghawanmeh, "The Position of the Islamic Action Front of the Political Process in the Period (1993–2013) in Jordan," *Research on Humanities and Social Sciences*, Vol. 4, No. 9, 2014.

Altz-Stamm, Amelia, "Jordan's Water Resource Challenges and the Prospects for Sustainability," unpublished manuscript, University of Texas, Austin, 2012. As of January 27, 2015: http://www.caee.utexas.edu/prof/maidment/giswr2012/TermPaper/Altz-Stamm.pdf

"'Amman Paper' Seeks to Safeguard Rights of Prisoners," *The Jordan Times*, November 9, 2013.

Amnesty International, *Growing Restrictions, Tough Conditions: The Plight of Those Fleeing Syria to Jordan*, London, October 30, 2013.

ANSA, "Aqaba Inks Deals to Build Gas, Petroleum Terminals," *ANSAMed*, November 4, 2013. As of January 27, 2015:
http://www.ansamed.info/ansamed/en/news/sections/economics/2013/11/04/ADC-signs-agreements-build-gas-petroleum-terminals_9565750.html

"Aqaba Residents to Have Greater Say in ASEZA Decisions," *The Jordan Times*, January 8, 2014. As of January 28, 2015:
http://jordantimes.com/aqaba-residents-to-have-greater-say-in-aseza-decisions

Arab Center for Research and Policy Studies, *Jordanian Public Perceptions of the Syrian Crisis*, Doha, Qatar, 2012. As of January 27, 2015:
http://english.dohainstitute.org/file/get/c5fb83ab-f280-4e24-b23f-15e803aae389.pdf

"Around 400 Syrians Enter Jordan on Monday," *The Jordan Times*, December 3, 2013. As of January 28, 2015:
http://jordantimes.com/around-400-syrians-enter-jordan-on-monday

Associated Press, "Jordan Jails Jihadist, Doctor for Aiding Syria Rebels," *Al-Arabiya*, November 6, 2013. As of January 27, 2015:
http://english.alarabiya.net/en/News/middle-east/2013/11/06/Jordanian-jails-Jihadist-doctor-for-aiding-Syria-rebels-.html

ATK, "ATK Completes First Flight Test of Its Light Gunship for Kingdom of Jordan," *PR Newswire*, December 4, 2013. As of January 28, 2015:
http://www.prnewswire.com/news-releases/atk-completes-first-flight-test-of-its-light-gunship-for-kingdom-of-jordan-234395931.html

Azzeh, Laila, "Initiative Launched to Combat Human Trafficking," *The Jordan Times*, December 9, 2013. As of January 27, 2015:
http://jordantimes.com/initiative-launched-to-combat-human-trafficking

Barhoumeh, Mohammad, "Jordan Threatened by Jihadist Spillover from Syria," *Al-Monitor*, April 25, 2014.

Bin Ali, Abdullah bin Hussein bin Talal bin Abdullah bin Hussein, "Our Journey to Forge Our Path Towards Democracy," discussion paper, Royal Hashemite Court, December 29, 2012. As of January 27, 2015:
http://kingabdullah.jo/index.php/en_US/pages/view/id/247.html

———, "Making Our Democratic System Work for All Jordanians," discussion paper, Royal Hashemite Court, January 16, 2013a. As of January 27, 2015:
http://kingabdullah.jo/index.php/en_US/pages/view/id/248.html

———, "Each Playing Our Part in a New Democracy," discussion paper, Royal Hashemite Court, March 2, 2013b. As of January 27, 2015:
http://kingabdullah.jo/index.php/en_US/pages/view/id/249.html

———, "Remarks by His Majesty King Abdullah II at the Closing Session of the World Economic Forum on the Middle East and North Africa, Dead Sea, Jordan," Royal Hashemite Court, May 26, 2013c. As of January 27, 2015:
http://kingabdullah.jo/index.php/en_US/speeches/view/id/520/videoDisplay/0.html

———, "Towards Democratic Empowerment and 'Active Citizenship,'" discussion paper, Royal Hashemite Court, June 2, 2013d. As of January 27, 2015:
http://kingabdullah.jo/index.php/en_US/pages/view/id/253.html

———, "Remarks by His Majesty King Abdullah II at 'Innovative Jordan' Conference, Berkeley, California," Royal Hashemite Court, May 13, 2014a. As of January 27, 2015:
http://kingabdullah.jo/index.php/en_US/speeches/view/id/541/videoDisplay/0.html

———, "Remarks by His Majesty King Abdullah II at the 9th World Islamic Economic Forum, London, UK," Royal Hashemite Court, October 29, 2014b. As of January 27, 2015:
http://kingabdullah.jo/index.php/en_US/speeches/view/id/530/videoDisplay/0.html

Bjawi-Levine, Laure, "My Heart Is Palestinian, My Passport Is Jordanian," in Rachel R. Reynolds, Cati Cole, Deborah A. Boehm, Joanna Dreby, Heather Rae-Espinoza, and Julia M. Hess, eds., *Emerging Perspectives on Children in Migratory Circumstances*, Philadelphia, Pa.: Drexel University Department of Culture and Communication and Drexel University College of Arts and Sciences, 2013, pp. 25–35. As of January 27, 2015: http://www.drexel.edu/culturecomm/contact/facultyDirectory/reynolds/cm_library/

Booth, William, and Taylor Luck, "Jordan Fears Homegrown ISIS More Than Invasion from Iraq," *Washington Post*, June 27, 2014. As of May 15, 2015: http://www.washingtonpost.com/world/middle_east/jordan-fears-homegrown-isis-more-than-invasion-from-iraq/2014/06/27/1534a4ee-f48a-492a-99b3-b6cd3ffe9e41_story.html

Browne, Evie, *Community Activism in Jordan*, Birmingham, United Kingdom: Governance and Social Development Resource Centre, University of Birmingham, GSDRC Helpdesk Research Report 957, 2013.

Burns, William J., "A Lot Has Changed but Not My Appreciation of Jordan's Role—Burns," *The Jordan Times*, January 28, 2014. As of January 28, 2015: http://jordantimes.com/a-lot-has-changed-but-not-my-appreciate-of-jordans-role---burns

Bush, Sarah Sunn, and Amaney A. Jamal, "Anti-Americanism, Authoritarian Politics, and Attitudes About Women's Representation: Evidence from a Survey Experiment in Jordan," *International Studies Quarterly*, Vol. 59, No. 1, March 2015, pp. 34–45. As of January 27, 2015: http://onlinelibrary.wiley.com/doi/10.1111/isqu.12139/abstract

CARE, *CARE Jordan Baseline Assessment of Community Identified Vulnerabilities Among Syrian Refugees Living in Amman*, research report, Amman, Jordan, 2012. As of January 28, 2015: http://data.unhcr.org/syrianrefugees/download.php?id=1177

Center for Strategic Studies, University of Jordan, "A Poll of Dr. Abdullah Ensour's Second Government 200 Days After Its Formation" (in Arabic), Amman, October 2013.

Chatelard, Geraldine, "Iraqis in Jordan: Elusive Numbers, Uncertain Future," *Viewpoints*, Washington, D.C.: The Middle East Institute, 2008.

Christophersen, Mona, "Protest and Reform in Jordan: Popular Demand and Government Response 2011 to 2012," Oslo, Norway: Fafo, 2013. As of January 28, 2015: http://www.fafo.no/index.php/nb/?option=com_zoo&task=item&item_id=6855&Itemid=923&lang=nb

Clover, Ian, "Yingli Solar Announces 1 MW of Accumulative Solar Shipments to Jordan," *PV Magazine*, November 19, 2013. As of January 28, 2015: http://www.pv-magazine.com/news/details/beitrag/yingli-solar-announces-1-mw-of-accumulative-solar-shipments-to-jordan_100013489/#axzz2llZFYzEg

Colthorpe, Andy, "Phoenix Solar to Build Jordan's First Megawatt-Scale PV Plant," *PV Tech*, December 13, 2013. As of January 30, 2015: http://www.pv-tech.org/news/phoenix_solar_to_build_jordans_first_megawatt_scale_pv_plant

CPI Financial, "Ratings on Kingdom of Jordan Affirmed at 'BB-/B'; Outlook Remains Negative," CPIFinancial.net, November 2, 2013. As of January 28, 2015: http://www.cpifinancial.net/news/post/23934/ratings-on-kingdom-of-jordan-affirmed-at-bb-b-outlook-remains-negative

Davis, Rochelle, and Abbie Taylor, *Syrian Refugees in Jordan and Lebanon: A Snapshot from Summer 2013*, Washington, D.C.: Center for Contemporary Arab Studies, Institute for the Study of International Migration, Georgetown University, 2013. As of January 28, 2015: https://georgetown.app.box.com/s/eifpeposkpxduunig816

"Decision on Nuclear Project Needs 20 Months—PM," *The Jordan Times*, January 9, 2014. As of January 28, 2015: http://jordantimes.com/decision-on-nuclear-project-needs-20-months----pm

Department of Statistics, *Jordan Statistical Yearbook for 2013* (Arabic and English), Amman, Jordan, 2013a. As of January 28, 2015: http://www.dos.gov.jo/dos_home_a/main/yearbook_2013.pdf

———, *Security and Justice*, Jordanian crime statistics, Amman, Jordan, 2013b.

"Development Plan to Create Jobs, Improve Tourism Services in Tafileh," *The Jordan Times*, December 9, 2013. As of January 29, 2015:
http://jordantimes.com/development-plan-to-create-jobs-improve-tourism-services-in-tafileh

Dhingra, Reva, "Syrian Refugees and the Jordanian Economy," *Muftah*, August 21, 2014. As of January 28, 2015:
http://muftah.org/syrian-refugees-jordanian-economy/#.VImUTYu4nUI

Duboisse, Laura, Alexis Everington, Tim Riesen, and Richard White, "Strategic and Operational Target Audience Analysis: The Hashemite Kingdom of Jordan," Amman, Jordan: Madison Springfield Incorporated, February 2014a.

———, "Strategic and Operational Target Audience Analysis in Jordan: Project Final Briefing," Amman, Jordan: Madison Springfield Incorporated, March 2014b.

Due-Gundersen, Nicolai, "Jordan's New Oil Sector: The Cyber Age of Hydrocarbon Security," *Proceedings of the International Conference on Computing Technology and Information Management*, Dubai, United Arab Emirates, 2014.

El-Said, Hamed, and Jane Harrigan, "Economic Reform, Social Welfare, and Instability: Jordan, Egypt, Morocco, and Tunisia, 1983–2004," *The Middle East Journal*, Vol. 68, No. 1, Winter 2014, pp. 99–121. As of January 28, 2015,
http://www.ingentaconnect.com/content/mei/mei/2014/00000068/00000001/art00006

"EU Mobilizes Another 85 Million Euros for Jordan, Syria," *The Jordan Times*, December 9, 2013.

Fanek, Fahed, "Jordan's Economy in 2014," *The Jordan Times*, December 1, 2013. As of January 28, 2015:
http://jordantimes.com/jordans-economy-in-2014

Freij, Muath, "Jordanians, Palestinians Voice Rejection of Kerry's Peace Plans," *The Jordan Times*, February 1, 2014. As of January 28, 2015:
http://jordantimes.com/jordanians-palestinians-voice-rejection-of-kerrys-peace-plans

Friedman, Jeffrey A., and Richard Zeckhauser, "Assessing Uncertainty in Intelligence," *Intelligence and National Security*, Vol. 27, No. 6, 2012, pp. 824–847.

———, "Handling and Mishandling Estimative Probability: Likelihood, Confidence, and the Search for Bin Laden," *Intelligence and National Security*, Vol. 30, No. 1, February 2015, pp. 77–99.

"German Support to Cover Kingdom's Water Sector," *The Jordan Times*, November 18, 2013. As of January 29, 2015:
http://jordantimes.com/german-support-to-cover-kingdoms-water-sector

"Germany to Finance Climate Protection Project Through 20m Euros Loan," *The Jordan Times*, December 23, 2013. As of January 29, 2015:
http://jordantimes.com/germany-to-finance-climate-protection-project-through-20m-euros-loan

Gharaybeh, Ibrahim, "Jordan's Economic Imbalance," *Al-Monitor*, October 30, 2013. As of January 28, 2015:
http://www.al-monitor.com/pulse/politics/2013/10/jordan-economic-policies-reform.html

Gharaybeh, Khlaif, "General Socio-Demographic Characteristics of the Jordanian Society: A Study in Social Geography," *Research on Humanities and Social Sciences*, Vol. 4, No. 1, 2014, pp. 1–10.

Ghazal, Mohammad, "Preparations Under Way to Build Central Badia Dam," *The Jordan Times*, October 31, 2013a. As of January 28, 2015:
http://jordantimes.com/preparations-under-way-to-build-central-badia-dam

———, "Newspapers Need Government Help to Avert Potential Closures," *The Jordan Times*, November 10, 2013b. As of January 28, 2015:
http://jordantimes.com/newspapers-need-govt-help-to-avert-potential-closures

———, "Islamists Should Show Good Faith by Committing to Openness," *Jordan Vista*, November 17, 2013c. As of January 28, 2015:
http://vista.sahafi.jo/art.php?id=217043c8b5b47228047e6bd850567c0147e340f4

———, "USAID Launches Jordan Competitiveness Programme," *Jordan Vista*, November 17, 2013d. As of January 28, 2015:
http://vista.sahafi.jo/art.php?id=1ea3efdcd713532c08535843bf5fea102f1c60e9

———, "Project Seeks to Allow Households to Generate Electricity," *The Jordan Times*, December 29, 2013e. As of January 28, 2015:
http://jordantimes.com/project-seeks-to-allow-households-to-generate-electricity

———, "State Security Court Releases Detained Journalists on Bail," *The Jordan Times*, December 31, 2013f. As of January 28, 2015:
http://jordantimes.com/state-security-court-releases-detained-journalists-on-bail

———, "IT Students Lack Training on Cyber Security," *The Jordan Times*, January 20, 2014. As of January 28, 2015:
http://jordantimes.com/it-students-lack-training-on-cyber-security----intj

Global Observatory, *Catalogue of Indices*, website, International Peace Institute, September 19, 2012. As of January 28, 2015:
http://theglobalobservatory.org/2012/09/indices/

GoJ—*See* Government of Jordan.

Government of Jordan, "Keys to the Kingdom: Government," web page, the Office of King Hussein I, Royal Hashemite Court, undated. As of January 28, 2015:
http://www.kinghussein.gov.jo/government.html

Greenwood, Scott, "Water Insecurity, Climate Change and Governance in the Arab World," *Middle East Policy*, Vol. 21, No. 2, Summer 2014, pp. 140–156.

Haddaw, Adel A., and Mahdy S. Othman, "The Impact of Some Economic Factors on Imports in Jordan," *The Research Journal of Finance and Accounting*, Vol. 4, No. 15, 2013.

Hafferkamp, Jonathan, "Reframing Youth Apathy in Jordan: An Anarchist Approach to Politics in the Hashemite Kingdom," thesis, Duke University, 2014.

Hamid, Shadi, and Courtney Freer, "How Stable Is Jordan? King Abdullah's Half-Hearted Reforms and the Challenge of the Arab Spring," Brookings Doha Center, November 2011.

Hansen, Ditte Ingemann, and Elsa Annaklara Eriksson, "The Arab Spring in Jordan: Social Movements and the Quest for Change," master's thesis, Roskilde University, 2013.

"Hashed Calls for Legislation That Serves Social Justice," *The Jordan Times*, November 26, 2013. As of January 29, 2015:
http://jordantimes.com/hashed-calls-for-legislation-that-serves-social-justice

Helmer, Olaf, *Analysis of the Future: The Delphi Method*, Santa Monica, Calif.: RAND Corporation, P-3558, March 1967. As of January 28, 2015:
http://www.rand.org/pubs/papers/P3558.html

Hiyari, Samir, and Samir Barhoum, "Interview with His Majesty King Abdullah II," Royal Hashemite Court, December 5, 2012. As of January 28, 2015:
http://kingabdullah.jo/index.php/en_US/interviews/view/id/501/videoDisplay/0.html

Hourani, Najib B., "Neoliberal Urbanism and the Arab Uprisings: A View from Amman," *Journal of Urban Affairs*, Vol. 36, No. S2, August 2014, pp. 650–662.

Human Rights Watch, "Jordan: End Trials of Protestors for 'Undermining Regime,'" October 29, 2013. As of January 28, 2015:
http://www.hrw.org/news/2013/10/29/jordan-end-trials-protesters-undermining-regime

Iaria, Vanessa, "Post-Return Transnationalism and the Iraqi Displacement in Syria and Jordan," *International Migration*, November 20, 2013.

Ibrahim, Mo'Awiyah, James Abbot Sauer, and Khair Yassine, "The East Jordan Valley Survey, 1975," *Bulletin of the American Schools of Oriental Research*, No. 222, 1976, pp. 41–66.

Identity Center and Netherlands Institute for Multiparty Democracy, *Map of the Political Parties and Movements in Jordan 2013/14*, Amman, Jordan, 2014.

ILO—*See* International Labour Organization.

"ILO Launches Project to Enhance Employment in Mafraq, Ibrid," *The Jordan Times*, November 14, 2013. As of January 29, 2015:
http://jordantimes.com/ilo-launches-project-to-enhance-employment-in-mafraq-irbid

"IMF Releases $261M Loan Tranche to Jordan," *The Jordan Times*, November 9, 2013. As of January 29, 2015:
http://jordantimes.com/imf-releases-261m-loan-tranche-to-jordan

"Inflation up by 5.6% in 2013 — Report," *The Jordan Times*, January 9, 2014. As of January 29, 2015:
http://jordantimes.com/inflation-up-by-56-in-2013----report

Integrated Regional Information Network, "Jordan: Bangladeshi Workers Protest Against Abuse," October 2, 2006. As of January 28, 2015:
http://www.irinnews.org/report/61858/jordan-bangladeshi-workers-protest-against-abuse

International Labour Organization, *Decent Work Country Programme, 2012–2015: Jordan*, Beirut, March 2012.

Jabbar, Sinaria Abdel, and Haidar Ibrahim Zaza, "Impact of Conflict in Syria on Syrian Children at the Zaatari Refugee Camp in Jordan," *Early Childhood Development and Care*, Vol. 184, Nos. 9–10, June 2014, pp. 1507–1530.

Jones, Ryan, "US, Jordan Agree: Israel Should Control Jordan Valley," *Israel Today*, December 9, 2013. As of January 28, 2015:
http://www.israeltoday.co.il/Default.aspx?tabid=178&nid=24298

"Jordan, EU Launch Negotiations for Free Trade Agreement," *The Jordan Times*, December 4, 2013. As of January 29, 2015:
http://jordantimes.com/jordan-eu-launch-negotiations-for-free-trade-agreement

"Jordan, Germany Ink Economic Assistance Deal," *The Jordan Times*, December 11, 2013. As of January 29, 2015:
http://jordantimes.com/jordan-germany-ink-economic-assistance-deal

"Jordan, Iraq Renew Commitment to Completing Vital Joint Projects," *The Jordan Times*, December 26, 2013. As of January 29, 2015:
http://jordantimes.com/jordan-iraq-renew-commitment-to-completing-vital-joint-projects

"Jordan Calls for Action Against Israeli Renovation at Jerusalem Holy Site," *The Jordan Times*, November 10, 2013. As of January 29, 2015:
http://jordantimes.com/jordan-calls-for-action-against-israeli-renovation-at-jerusalem-holy-site

"Jordan Calls for Speeding Up Implementation of Iraq Pipeline," *The Jordan Times*, January 9, 2014. As of January 29, 2015:
http://jordantimes.com/jordan-calls-for-speeding-up-implementation-of-iraq-pipeline

"Jordanian-American Jihadist Detained," *The Jordan Times*, December 4, 2013.

"Jordanian-Saudi Military Exercise Wraps Up in Tabuk," *Ammon News*, November 22, 2013. As of January 27, 2015:
http://en.ammonnews.net/article.aspx?articleno=23659#.UpTDDY2MWFE

"Jordan Living Under Shadow of Potential Arab Spring," *Ammon News*, November 4, 2013.

"Jordan Needs $3.2 Billion to Deal with Impact of Syria Crisis in 2014," *Ammon News*, November 4, 2013.

Jordan Reform Watch, *Reform in Jordan: Report #8*, Amman, Jordan, 2012.

"Jordan to Try for UN Security Council Seat Saudi Arabia Declined," *Voice of Russia*, November 13, 2013. As of February 2, 2015:
http://sputniknews.com/voiceofrussia/2013_11_13/
Jordan-to-try-for-UN-Security-Council-seat-Saudi-Arabia-declined-5810/

"Jordan Urges Israel to Remove Aqsa Surveillance Cameras," *Al Bawaba*, December 18, 2013. As of January 27, 2015:
http://www.albawaba.com/news/jordan-aqsa-surveillance--541413

"Jordan Wins UN Security Council Seat," *The Jordan Times*, December 6, 2013. As of January 29, 2015:
http://jordantimes.com/jordan-wins-un-security-council-seat

"JPF Employees Give Government 48 Hours to Meet Their Demands," *The Jordan Times*, November 17, 2013. As of January 29, 2015:
http://jordantimes.com/jpf-employees-give-government-48-hours-to-meet-their-demands

"JPF Employees to Strike on Monday," *The Jordan Times*, November 9, 2013. As of January 29, 2015:
http://jordantimes.com/jpf-employees-to-strike-on-monday

Kent, Sherman, "Words of Estimative Probability," *Studies in Intelligence*, Central Intelligence Agency, 1964. As of January 29, 2015:
https://www.cia.gov/library/center-for-the-study-of-intelligence/csi-publications/books-and-monographs/sherman-kent-and-the-board-of-national-estimates-collected-essays/6words.html

Khrawish, Husni Ali, "The Effect of Economic and Financial Risks on Foreign Direct Investment in Jordan: Multivariate Analysis," *International Business Research*, Vol. 7, No. 5, 2014, pp. 124–136.

Kimmelman, Michael, "Refugee Camp for Syrians in Jordan Evolves as a Do-It-Yourself City," *The New York Times*, July 4, 2014. As of January 29, 2015:
http://www.nytimes.com/2014/07/05/world/middleeast/zaatari-refugee-camp-in-jordan-evolves-as-a-do-it-yourself-city.html?_r=0

"Kingdom 'Resentful' at Inadequate International Aid to Refugees," *The Jordan Times*, January 7, 2014. As of January 29, 2015:
http://jordantimes.com/kingdom-resentful-at-inadequate-intl-aid-to-refugees

Koprulu, Nur, "Jordan Since the Uprisings: Between Change and Stability," *Middle East Policy*, Vol. 21, No. 2, Summer 2014, pp. 111–126.

Krasner, JanSuzane, "Arab Spring Fever in Jordan," *American Thinker*, January 12, 2014. As of January 29, 2015:
http://www.americanthinker.com/blog/2014/01/arab_spring_fever_in_jordan.html

Kuttab, Daoud, "Licensing a News Website," *The Jordan Times*, November 6, 2013a. As of January 29, 2015:
http://jordantimes.com/licensing-a-news-website

———, "Decentralization Has Benefits," *The Jordan Times*, November 13, 2013b. As of January 29, 2015:
http://jordantimes.com/decentralisation-has-benefits

———, "Jordan and the Palestinian Refugees," *The Jordan Times*, January 22, 2014. As of March 28, 2015:
http://jordantimes.com/jordan-and-the-palestinian-refugees

"Kuwait Fund to Finance Aqaba's Liquid Natural Gas Terminal," *Gazzetta del Sud*, November 20, 2013. As of January 28, 2015:
http://www.gazzettadelsud.it/news/english/69690/Kuwait-Fund-to-finance-Aqaba-s-Liquid-Natural-Gas-Terminal.html

Laub, Karin, and Mohammed Daraghmeh, "Largest Camp for Syrian Refugees Becoming a City," Associated Press via *The Jordan Times*, November 7, 2013. As of January 29, 2015:
http://jordantimes.com/largest-camp-for-syrian-refugees-becoming-a-city

Leigh, Karen, "Domestic Violence on the Rise Among Syrian Refugees," *The New York Times*, August 29, 2014. As of January 29, 2015:
http://kristof.blogs.nytimes.com/2014/08/29/domestic-violence-on-the-rise-among-syrian-refugees/?_r=0

"Local Company to Resume Gas Exploration After BP Bows Out," *The Jordan Times*, January 18, 2014. As of January 29, 2015:
http://jordantimes.com/local-company-to-resume-gas-exploration-after-bp-bows-out

Luck, Taylor, "Russian Firm Set to Build Jordan's First Nuclear Plants," *The Jordan Times*, October 28, 2013a. As of January 29, 2015:
http://jordantimes.com/russian-firm-set-to-build-jordans-first-nuclear-plants

———, "Jordan Refutes Amnesty Claims, Says Border Open to Syrian Refugees," *The Jordan Times*, October 31, 2013b. As of January 29, 2015:
http://jordantimes.com/jordan-refutes-amnesty-claims-says-border-open-to-syrian-refugees

———, "Protesters Call for Government Resignation," *The Jordan Times*, November 2, 2013c. As of January 29, 2015:
http://jordantimes.com/protesters-call-for-govt-resignation

———, "400 Syrians Flee to Jordan amid Border Siege," *The Jordan Times*, November 6, 2013d. As of January 29, 2015:
http://jordantimes.com/400-syrians-flee-to-jordan-amid-border-siege

———, "Syrian Flight to Jordan Builds amid Border Battle," *The Jordan Times*, November 7, 2013e. As of January 29, 2015:
http://jordantimes.com/syrian-flight-to-jordan-builds-amid-border-battle

———, "Central Badia Residents Denounce Nuclear Reactor Plans," *The Jordan Times*, November 9, 2013f. As of January 29, 2015:
http://jordantimes.com/central-badia-residents-denounce-nuclear-reactor-plans

———, "Hundreds of Syrians Flee to Jordan amid Refugee Camp Delays," *The Jordan Times*, November 9, 2013g. As of January 29, 2015:
http://jordantimes.com/hundreds-of-syrians-flee-to-jordan-amid-refugee-camp-delays

———, "Over 1,000 Syrians Entered Jordan over Past 72 Hours," *The Jordan Times*, November 10, 2013h. As of January 29, 2015:
http://jordantimes.com/over-1000-syrians-entered-jordan-over-past-72-hours

———, "Two Jordanians Jailed for Syrian Jihadist Ties," *Jordan Vista*, November 12, 2013i. As of May 15, 2015:
http://vista.sahafi.jo/art.php?id=e700b8250646a9618deda75e61854525d9fd4d4d

———, "Over 1,000 Syrian Refugees Enter Jordan on Thursday," *The Jordan Times*, November 14, 2013j. As of January 29, 2015:
http://jordantimes.com/over-1000-syrian-refugees-enter-jordan-on-thursday

———, "Activists Protest Against Rising Prices," *The Jordan Times*, November 16, 2013k. As of January 29, 2015:
http://jordantimes.com/Activists+protest+against+rising+prices-66637

———, "Tribesmen, Azraq Residents 'Say No' to Nuclear Reactor Location," *The Jordan Times*, November 16, 2013l. As of January 29, 2015:
http://jordantimes.com/tribesmen-azraq-residents-say-no-to-nuclear-reactor-location

———, "Hundreds of Syrians Flee to Jordan," *The Jordan Times*, November 21, 2013m. As of January 29, 2015:
http://jordantimes.com/hundreds-of-syrians-flee-to-jordan

———, "Protesters Mark Anniversary of November Fuel Riots," *The Jordan Times*, November 23, 2013n. As of January 29, 2015:
http://jordantimes.com/protesters-mark-anniversary-of-november-fuel-riots

———, "Jordan Renews Al-Aqsa Warnings," *The Jordan Times*, November 24, 2013o. As of January 29:
http://jordantimes.com/jordan-renews-al-aqsa-warnings

———, "Dozens of Injured Syrians Enter Jordan," *The Jordan Times*, November 25, 2013p. As of January 29, 2015:
http://jordantimes.com/dozens-of-injured-syrians-enter-jordan

———, "Jordan Energy Demand 'Outpacing Supply,' Officials Warn," *The Jordan Times*, November 25, 2013q. As of January 29, 2015:
http://jordantimes.com/jordan-energy-demand-outpacing-supply-officials-warn

———, "Injured Syrians Seek Treatment in Jordan," *The Jordan Times*, November 26, 2013r. As of January 29, 2015:
http://jordantimes.com/injured-syrians-seek-treatment-in-jordan

———, "Jordan Closing in on Vendor of First Oil Shale Plant," *The Jordan Times*, November 26, 2013s. As of January 29, 2015:
http://mideastenvironment.apps01.yorku.ca/2013/11/jordan-closing-in-on-vendor-of-first-oil-shale-plant-jordan-times/

———, "Badia Residents Protest Against Nuclear Reactor," *The Jordan Times*, November 28, 2013t. As of January 29, 2015:
http://jordantimes.com/badia-residents-protest-against-nuclear-reactor

———, "128 Jordanians 'Slain' in Syria—Report," *The Jordan Times*, November 30, 2013u. As of January 29, 2015:
http://jordantimes.com/128-jordanians-slain-in-syria----report

———, "Syrian Refugees to Cost Jordan 'over $2 Billion,'" *The Jordan Times,* December 5, 2013v. As of January 29, 2015:
http://jordantimes.com/syrian-refugees-to-cost-jordan-over-2-billion

———, "Hundreds of Syrians Flee to Jordan amid Fresh Chemical Massacre Claims," *The Jordan Times*, December 7, 2013w. As of January 29, 2015:
http://jordantimes.com/hundreds-of-syrians-flee-to-jordan-amid-fresh-chemical-massacre-claims

———, "Syrian Exodus to Jordan Grows amid Aerial Strikes," *The Jordan Times*, December 8, 2013x. As of January 29, 2015:
http://jordantimes.com/syrian-exodus-to-jordan-grows-amid-aerial-strikes

———, "Hundreds of Syrians Flee to Jordan amid Thawing Temperatures," *The Jordan Times*, December 21, 2013y. As of January 29, 2015:
http://jordantimes.com/hundreds-of-syrians-flee-to-jordan-amid-thawing-temperatures

———, "Protestors Demand Government Resignation over High Prices," *The Jordan Times,* December 21, 2013z. As of January 29, 2015:
http://jordantimes.com/protesters-demand-govt-resignation-over-high-prices

———, "600 Syrians Flee to Jordan on Tuesday," *The Jordan Times*, December 24, 2013aa. As of January 29, 2015:
http://jordantimes.com/600-syrians-flee-to-jordan-on-Tuesday

———, "Jordanian Jihadist Killed in Syria," *The Jordan Times*, December 24, 2013bb.

———, "500 Syrians Enter Jordan as Border Fighting Continues," *The Jordan Times*, December 30, 2013cc. As of January 29, 2015:
http://jordantimes.com/500-syrians-enter-jordan-as-border-fighting-continues

———, "Over 200 Jordanian Jihadists Killed in Syria," *Jordan Vista*, December 30, 2013dd. As of January 29, 2015:
http://vista.sahafi.jo/art.php?id=436fdf2c56c6687adef3c8850a33742b36b3e7cf

———, "Border Fighting Drives Hundreds of Syrians into Jordan," *The Jordan Times*, January 4, 2014a. As of January 29, 2015:
http://jordantimes.com/border-fighting-drives-hundreds-of-syrians-into-jordan

———, "Refugee Flight to Jordan Builds as Border Bombardment Continues," *The Jordan Times*, January 6, 2014b. As of January 29, 2015:
http://jordantimes.com/refugee-flight-to-jordan-builds-as-border-bombardment-continues

———, "Detained Islamists Begin Hunger Strike," *Jordan Vista*, February 3, 2014c. As of January 29, 2015:
http://vista.sahafi.jo/art.php?id=2aaa9444905823dd11f034b5c89a2c7a449431bb

Lust-Okar, Ellen, "Elections Under Authoritarianism: Preliminary Lessons from Jordan," *Democratization*, Vol. 13, No. 3, 2006, pp. 456–471.

Ma'ayeh, Suha Philip, "Jordanian Jihadists Active in Syria," Combating Terrorism Center at West Point, October 24, 2013. As of January 29, 2015:
https://www.ctc.usma.edu/posts/jordanian-jihadists-active-in-syria

MacBride, Elizabeth, "The Syria Business Uprising," CNBC.com, December 6, 2013. As of January 29, 2015:
http://www.cnbc.com/id/101229717#

Malkawi, Khetam, "UN to Address Jordan's Development Needs Amidst Refugee Crisis," *The Jordan Times*, November 4, 2013. As of January 29, 2015:
http://jordantimes.com/un-to-address-jordans-development-needs-amidst-refugee-crisis

———, "Vaccination Campaign Reaches 29% of Targeted Group by Fourth Day," *The Jordan Times*, November 6, 2013. As of January 29, 2015:
http://jordantimes.com/vaccination-campaign-reaches-29-of-targeted-group-by-fourth-day

———, "UNHCR Preparing 'Winterisation Programme' for Syrian Refugees," *The Jordan Times*, November 16, 2013. As of January 29, 2015:
http://jordantimes.com/unhcr-preparing-winterisation-programme-for-syrian-refugees

———, "Jordan Officially Applies to Security Council Seat," *The Jordan Times*, November 18, 2013. As of January 29, 2015:
http://jordantimes.com/jordan-officially-applies-to-security-council-seat

———, "Vaccination Campaign Extended to Reach All Schools in Amman," *The Jordan Times*, November 21, 2013. As of January 29, 2015:
http://jordantimes.com/vaccination-campaign-extended-to-reach-all-schools-in-amman

———, "Nationwide Vaccination Campaign Concludes," *The Jordan Times*, November 25, 2013. As of January 29, 2015:
http://jordantimes.com/nationwide-vaccination-campaign-concludes

———, "HIV/AIDS Cases in Jordan at Risk of Increasing amid Refugee Waves," *The Jordan Times*, December 1, 2013. As of January 29, 2015:
http://jordantimes.com/hivaids-cases-in-jordan-at-risk-of-increasing-amid-refugee-waves

———, "New Campaign Aimed at Immunizing 1M Children Against Polio," *The Jordan Times*, December 22, 2013. As of January 29, 2015:
http://jordantimes.com/new-campaign-aimed-at-immunising-1m-children-against-polio

———, "Jordan Will Not Label Brotherhood as Terrorist Group, Egypt Style' Minister," *The Jordan Times*, December 28, 2013. As of January 29, 2015:
http://jordantimes.com/jordan-will-not-label-brotherhood-as-terrorist-group-egypt-style-minister

———, "Gov't Notified over Egypt Request to Enforce Anti-Terror Pan-National Deal," *The Jordan Times*, January 2, 2014. As of January 29, 2015:
http://jordantimes.com/govt-notified-over-egypt-request-to-enforce-anti-terror-pan-national-deal

———, "Mansour Says Jordan's Islamists Will Likely Survive 'Regional Conspiracy,'" *Jordan Vista*, January 2, 2014. As of January 29, 2015:
http://vista.sahafi.jo/art.php?id=88f331637f8ed8d430c3acdd272cc17e4202f54b

———, "Impact of Refugees on Jordan 'Immeasurable' at Present—Expert," *The Jordan Times*, January 5, 2014. As of January 29, 2015:
http://jordantimes.com/impact-of-refugees-on-jordan-immeasurable-at-present----expert

———, "Second Vaccination Campaign Concludes," *The Jordan Times*, January 5, 2014. As of January 29, 2015:
http://jordantimes.com/second-vaccination-campaign-concludes

———, "Al Qaeda-Linked ISIL No Threat to Jordan," *The Jordan Times*, January 6, 2014. As of January 29, 2015:
http://jordantimes.com/%E2%80%98Al+Qaeda-linked+ISIL+no+threat+to+Jordan%E2%80%99-68301

———, "Number of Registered Syrian Refugees Reaches 585,656—UNHCR," *The Jordan Times*, January 20, 2014. As of January 29, 2015:
http://jordantimes.com/number-of-registered-syrian-refugees-reaches-585656----unhcr

———, "HRW Criticizes Press Law, 'Failure' to Amend Penal Code to Guarantee Free Speech," *The Jordan Times*, January 25, 2014. As of January 29, 2015:
http://jordantimes.com/hrw-criticises-press-law-failure-to-amend-penal-code-to-guarantee-free-speech

———, "Kingdom's Exports to Ukraine Drop by Half Due to Syrian Crisis," *The Jordan Times*, January 28, 2014. As of January 29, 2015:
http://jordantimes.com/kingdoms-exports-to-ukraine-drop-by-half-due-to-syrian-crisis

Mercy Corps, *Analysis of Host Community-Refugee Tensions in Mafraq, Jordan*, October 2012. As of January 29, 2015:
http://www.alnap.org/resource/8676

Migration Policy Centre, "Migration Facts Jordan," web page, April 2013. As of January 29, 2015:
http://www.migrationpolicycentre.eu/docs/fact_sheets/Factsheet%20Jordan.pdf

Ministry of Planning and International Cooperation, *Jordan Response Plan 2015 for the Syria Crisis*, final draft, Amman, Jordan: Hashemite Kingdom of Jordan, 2014. As of May 11, 2015:
http://www.jo.undp.org/content/dam/jordan/docs/Publications/JRP+Final+Draft+2014.12.17.pdf

Ministry of Water and Irrigation, *Water for Life: Jordan's Water Strategy 2008–2022*, Amman, Jordan: Hashemite Kingdom of Jordan, 2009.

———, "Red Dead Sea Project," Hashemite Kingdom of Jordan, undated. As of January 28, 2015:
http://www.jva.gov.jo/sites/en-us/RSDS/default.aspx

"Mobile Penetration Reaches 155%," *The Jordan Times*, December 4, 2013. As of January 29, 2015:
http://jordantimes.com/mobile-penetration-reaches-155

Mohaddes, Kamiar, and Mehdi Raissi, *Oil Prices, External Income, and Growth: Lessons from Jordan*, International Monetary Fund, Working Paper 11/291, December 2011. As of January 29, 2015:
http://www.imf.org/external/pubs/ft/wp/2011/wp11291.pdf

Mowafi, Hani, and Paul Spiegel, "The Iraqi Refugee Crisis: Familiar Problems and New Challenges," *Journal of the American Medical Association*, Vol. 299, No. 14, May 2008, pp. 1713–1715.

Mufti, Malik, "Elite Bargains and the Onset of Political Liberalization in Jordan," *Comparative Political Studies*, Vol. 32, No. 1, February 1999, pp. 100–129.

Muhtaseb, Lamis, *Jordan's East Banker-Palestinian Schism*, Oslo: Norwegian Peacebuilding Resource Centre, 2013.

Namrouqa, Hana, "Ministry to Evaluate Syrian Refugee Impact on Water Sector," *The Jordan Times*, November 4, 2013a. As of January 30, 2015:
http://jordantimes.com/ministry-to-evaluate-syrian-refugee-impact-on-water-sector

———, "Disi Project Now Operating at 90% of Capacity—Nasser," *The Jordan Times*, November 5, 2013b. As of January 30, 2015:
http://jordantimes.com/disi-project-now-operating-at-90-of-capacity----nasser

———, "Construction of Pipeline to Supply Northern Region with Disi Water Begins in Q2 of 2014," *The Jordan Times*, November 7, 2013c. As of January 30, 2015:
http://jordantimes.com/construction-of-pipeline-to-supply-northern-region-with-disi-water-begins-in-q2-of-2014

———, "South Amman Wastewater Treatment Plant to Start Partial Operations Next Year," *The Jordan Times*, November 12, 2013d. As of January 30, 2015:
http://jordantimes.com/south-amman-wastewater-treatment-plant-to-start-partial-operations-next-year

———, "Authorities to Revamp Irbid's Water Networks," *The Jordan Times*, November 19, 2013e. As of January 29, 2015:
http://jordantimes.com/authorities-to-revamp-irbids-water-networks

———, "Ain Ghazal Wastewater Treatment Plant to Be Revamped," *The Jordan Times*, November 20, 2013f. As of January 29, 2015:
http://jordantimes.com/ain-ghazal-wastewater-treatment-plant-to-be-revamped

———, “Water Cooperation Needed for Secure World—Report,” *The Jordan Times*, November 25, 2013g. As of January 30, 2015:
http://jordantimes.com/water-cooperation-needed-for-secure-world----report

———, “Zarqa Water Situation to Improve Within Three Years,” *The Jordan Times*, November 26, 2013h. As of January 30, 2015:
http://jordantimes.com/zarqa-water-situation-to-improve-within-three-years

———, “Water Projects Worth JD3.3 Million to Be Implemented in Northern, Eastern Regions,” *The Jordan Times*, December 3, 2013i.

———, “Jordan Signs Deal with Palestine, Israel to Implement Phase 1 of Red-Dead Project,” *The Jordan Times*, December 9, 2013j. As of January 30, 2015:
http://jordantimes.com/jordan-signs-deal-with-palestine-israel-to-implement-phase-i-of-red-dead-project

———, “Project Launched to Revamp Water Networks in Madaba,” *The Jordan Times*, December 26, 2013k. As of January 30, 2015:
http://jordantimes.com/project-launched-to-revamp-water-networks-in-madaba

———, “Authorities to Revamp Ajloun Water Networks,” *The Jordan Times*, December 30, 2013l. As of January 29, 2015:
http://jordantimes.com/authorities-to-revamp-ajloun-water-networks

———, “Kufranjah Wastewater Treatment Plant Expansion to Conclude This Year,” *The Jordan Times*, January 2, 2014a. As of January 30, 2015:
http://jordantimes.com/kufranjah-wastewater-treatment-plant-expansion-to-conclude-this-year

———, “Construction of Main Water Conveyors for Ajloun, Jerash Starts,” *The Jordan Times*, January 4, 2014b. As of January 30, 2015:
http://jordantimes.com/construction-of-main-water-conveyors-for-ajloun-jerash-starts

———, “Qualifying Firms for Red-Dead Project to Be Announced This Year—Nasser,” *The Jordan Times*, January 7, 2014c. As of January 30, 2015:
http://jordantimes.com/qualifying-firms-for-red-dead-project-to-be-announced-this-year---nasser

———, “Over 800 Institutions Closed Last Year for Violating Labour Law,” *The Jordan Times*, January 15, 2014d. As of January 30, 2015:
http://jordantimes.com/over-800-institutions-closed-last-year-for-violating-labour-law

———, “Pumping from Disi at Full Capacity Begins,” *The Jordan Times*, January 18, 2014e. As of January 30, 2015:
http://jordantimes.com/pumping-from-disi-at-full-capacity-begins

———, “Conservationists Call for Regulating Wind Energy Projects to Protect Wildlife,” *The Jordan Times*, January 30, 2014f. As of January 30, 2015:
http://jordantimes.com/conservationists-call-for-regulating-wind-energy-projects-to-protect-wildlife

Nashashibi, Sharif, “Why Peace with Israel Was Good for Jordan,” *Al-Jazeera*, October 26, 2014. As of January 30, 2015:
http://www.aljazeera.com/indepth/opinion/2014/10/why-peace-with-israel-was-good--201410265360338272.html

Neimat, Khaled, “MP-Led Reform Initiative ‘Gains Momentum,’” *The Jordan Times*, November 2, 2013a. As of January 30, 2015:
http://jordantimes.com/article/mp-led-reform-initiative-gains-momentum

———, “Work on Iraq Pipeline to Start End of January,” *The Jordan Times*, December 29, 2013b. As of January 30, 2015:
http://jordantimes.com/work-on-iraq-pipeline-to-start-end-of-january----pm

———, “Lawmakers Call for Enlarging Army, Security Agencies amid Regional Threats,” *The Jordan Times*, January 7, 2014. As of January 30, 2015:
http://jordantimes.com/lawmakers-call-for-enlarging-army-security-agencies-amid-regional-threats

“New Electricity Tariff Effective at Year Turn,” *The Jordan Times*, December 31, 2013. As of January 29, 2015:
http://jordantimes.com/new-electricity-tariff-effective-at-year-turn

"New JPF Board Holds First Meeting," *The Jordan Times*, November 20, 2013. As of January 29, 2015:
http://jordantimes.com/new-jpf-board-holds-first-meeting

Nimry, Hana, "Water Stress in Jordan," *The Jordan Times*, December 29, 2013. As of January 30, 2015:
http://jordantimes.com/water-stress-in-jordan

Numan, Abeer, "Jordan, S. Arabia Sign $299.4M Deals to Finance Development Projects," *The Jordan Times*, February 8, 2013. As of January 30, 2015:
http://jordantimes.com/jordan-s-arabia-sign-2994m-deals-to-finance-development-projects

Obeidat, Omar, "Projects Worth JD486 Million to Be Implemented in Central Badia," *The Jordan Times*, October 28, 2013a. As of January 30, 2015:
http://jordantimes.com/projects-worth-jd486-million-to-be-implemented-in-central-badia

———, "Alaa Hammad Taken to Israeli Military Hospital," *The Jordan Times*, November 9, 2013b. As of January 30, 2015:
http://jordantimes.com/article/alaa-hammad-taken-to-israeli-military-hospital

———, "Al Rai Share Price up After Labour Protests Ended," *The Jordan Times*, November 13, 2013c. As of January 30, 2015:
http://jordantimes.com/al-rai-share-price-up-after-labour-protests-ended

———, "Gov't to Create More Jobs to Handle Refugee Influx," *The Jordan Times*, November 20, 2013d. As of January 30, 2015:
http://jordantimes.com/govt-to-create-more-jobs-to-handle-refugee-influx

———, "Ministry Reports Success in Measures to Control Labour Market," *The Jordan Times*, November 26, 2013e. As of January 30, 2015:
http://jordantimes.com/ministry-reports-success-in-measures-to-control-labour-market

———, "Think Tank Ranks Jordan Among Top Arab World's Economically Free States," *The Jordan Times*, November 30, 2013f. As of January 30, 2015:
http://jordantimes.com/think-tank-ranks-jordan-among-top-arab-worlds-economically-free-states

———, "Ad Dustour Sit-In Enters Second Day," *The Jordan Times*, December 3, 2013g. As of January 30, 2015:
http://jordantimes.com/ad-dustour-sit-in-enters-second-day

———, "96% of Operations at Aqaba Port 'Running Smoothly' as Workers Begin Strike," *The Jordan Times*, December 8, 2013h. As of January 30, 2015:
http://jordantimes.com/96-of-operations-at-aqaba-port-running-smoothly-as-workers-begin-strike

———, "Demand for Bread Doubles Ahead of Expected Snowstorm," *The Jordan Times*, December 11, 2013i. As of January 30, 2015:
http://jordantimes.com/demand-for-bread-doubles-ahead-of-expected-snowstorm

———, "Blizzard Paralyses Life in Jordan, to Ease Sunday," *The Jordan Times*, December 14, 2013j. As of January 30, 2015:
http://jordantimes.com/blizzard-paralyses-life-in-jordan-to-ease-sunday

———, "Iraq Closes Border with Jordan—Source," *The Jordan Times*, December 24, 2013k. As of January 30, 2015:
http://jordantimes.com/iraq-closes-border-with-jordan----source

———, "Planned Electricity Hikes to Badly Affect Industrial, Commercial Sectors," *The Jordan Times*, December 29, 2013l. As of January 30, 2015:
http://jordantimes.com/planned-electricity-hikes-to-badly-affect-industrial-commercial-sectors

———, "Authorities Release 3rd List of Guest Workers with Expired Permits," *The Jordan Times*, January 11, 2014a. As of January 30, 2015:
http://jordantimes.com/authorities-release-3rd-list-of-guest-workers-with-expired-permits

———, "Non-Jordanian Investors Position Amman Bourse on Rising Trajectory," *The Jordan Times*, January 14, 2014b. As of January 30, 2015:
http://jordantimes.com/non-jordanian-investors-position-amman-bourse-on-rising-trajectory

———, "Slumping Oil Prices Save Jordan Millions, 'But Not for Long,'" *The Jordan Times*, October 29, 2014c. As of January 30, 2015:
http://jordantimes.com/slumping-oil-prices-save-jordan-millions-but-not-for-long

Oddone, Elisa, "Displaced Syrian Women Struggle to Make a Living in Host Communities," *The Jordan Times*, November 14, 2013. As of January 30, 2015:
http://elisaoddone.com/2013/11/15/displaced-syrian-women-struggle-to-make-a-living-in-host-communities/

Oksam, Matt, "The Syrian Refugee Crisis and the Jordan Border Security Program (JBSP)," *CECOM Dots and Dashes*, September 2013. As of October 28, 2014:
http://www.cecom.army.mil/DOTS-N-DASHES/2013/SEPTEMBER/files/assets/common/downloads/page0001.pdf

Olwan, Mohamed Y., "The Legal Framework of Forced Migration and Refugee Movements in Jordan," discussion paper, Forced Migration and Refugee Studies Program, American University in Cairo, Egypt, October 2007. As of January 30, 2015:
http://www.aucegypt.edu/GAPP/cmrs/Documents/MohamedOlwan.pdf

Olwan, Mohamed Y., and Ahmad Shiyab, "Forced Migration of Syrians to Jordan: An Exploratory Study," San Domenico di Fiesole, Italy: Migration Policy Centre, Robert Schuman Centre for Advanced Studies, European University Institute, 2012. As of January 30, 2015:
http://cadmus.eui.eu/bitstream/handle/1814/23502/MPC-RR-2012-06.pdf

Omari, Raed, "EU Allocates 180M Euros to Assist Jordan," *The Jordan Times*, November 26, 2013a. As of January 30, 2015:
http://jordantimes.com/eu-allocates-180m-euros-to-assist-jordan

———, "Jordanian Suspends Hunger Strike in Israel," *The Jordan Times*, December 4, 2013b. As of January 30, 2015:
http://jordantimes.com/jordanian-suspends-hunger-strike-in-israel

———, "Preparations Under Way for Visits to Jordanians in Israel Jails," *The Jordan Times*, December 8, 2013c. As of January 30, 2015:
http://jordantimes.com/preparations-under-way-for-visits-to-jordanians-in-israel-jails

———, "UJ Launches MA Program in Sustainable Development," *The Jordan Times*, January 8, 2014a. As of January 30, 2015:
http://jordantimes.com/uj-launches-ma-programme-in-sustainable-development

———, "EU Helps Jordan Beef Up Security at Syrian Refugee Camps," *The Jordan Times*, January 16, 2014b. As of January 30, 2015:
http://jordantimes.com/eu-helps-jordan-beef-up-security-at-syrian-refugee-camps

O'Toole, Megan, "Discontent Simmers Among East Bank Jordanians," *Al-Jazeera English*, June 3, 2014. As of January 30, 2015:
http://www.aljazeera.com/news/middleeast/2014/06/discontent-simmers-among-east-bank-jordanians-20146381828614925.html

"Over 15,000 Illegal Guest Workers Apprehended Since August—Katamine," *The Jordan Times*, November 16, 2013. As of January 29, 2015:
http://jordantimes.com/over-15000-illegal-guest-workers-apprehended-since-august----katamine

Oxford Business Group, *The Report: Jordan 2013*, London: Oxford Business Group, 2013. As of January 30, 2015:
http://www.oxfordbusinessgroup.com/product/report/report-jordan-2013

"Palestine Supports Jordan's Red Sea Desalination Project—Abbas," *The Jordan Times*, November 24, 2013. As of January 29, 2015:
http://jordantimes.com/palestine-supports-jordans-red-sea-desalination-project----abbas

Parrish, Karen, "Dempsey Visits U.S. Troops Serving in Jordan," American Forces Press Service, U.S. Department of Defense, August 15, 2013. As of January 30, 2015:
http://www.defense.gov/news/newsarticle.aspx?id=120629

Partee, Barbara, "Model Semantics in National Intelligence Estimate," blog post, *Language Log*, University of Pennsylvania, December 4, 2007. As of January 30, 2015:
http://itre.cis.upenn.edu/~myl/languagelog/archives/005179.html

Petra News Agency, "Irbid Mayor Calls for More Support to Offset Refugee Burden," *The Jordan Times*, November 6, 2013a. As of January 30, 2015:
http://jordantimes.com/irbid-mayor-calls-for-more-support-to-offset-refugee-burden

———, "Remittances from Jordanian Expatriates Increase," *The Jordan Times*, November 16, 2013b. As of January 29, 2015:
http://jordantimes.com/remittances-from-jordanian-expatriates-increase

———, "Six-Day Vaccination Campaign Targets Zaatari Children," *The Jordan Times*, November 20, 2013c. As of January 30, 2015:
http://jordantimes.com/six-day-vaccination-campaign-targets-zaatari-children

———, "Syrians Charged with Smuggling Arms Plead Not Guilty," *The Jordan Times*, November 20, 2013d. As of January 30, 2015:
http://jordantimes.com/syrians-charged-with-smuggling-arms-plead-not-guilty

———, "Electricity Company Workers Observe Work Stoppage," *The Jordan Times*, November 21, 2013e. As of January 30, 2015:
http://jordantimes.com/electricity-company-workers-observe-work-stoppage

———, "Meetings Emphasise Need for Sanitary Services in Mafraq," *The Jordan Times*, November 23, 2013f. As of January 30, 2015:
http://jordantimes.com/meetings-emphasise-need-for-sanitary-services-in-mafraq

———, "Gov't to Support Efforts to Win Security Council Seat," *The Jordan Times*, November 24, 2013g. As of January 29, 2015:
http://jordantimes.com/govt-to-support-efforts-to-win-security-council-seat

———, "Ad Dustour Employees to 'Step up' Protest Action," *The Jordan Times*, November 30, 2013h. As of January 30, 2015:
http://jordantimes.com/ad-dustour-employees-to-step-up-protest-action

———, "Jordanian Child Diagnosed with MERS Virus in Abu Dhabi," *The Jordan Times*, December 1, 2013i. As of January 30, 2015:
http://jordantimes.com/jordanian-child-diagnosed-with-mers-virus-in-abu-dhabi

———, "Financial Difficulties Hampering State Media Work—Momani," *The Jordan Times*, December 5, 2013j. As of January 29, 2015:
http://jordantimes.com/financial-difficulties-hampering-state-media-work----momani

———, "Ensour Meets Delegates from US RAND Corporation," *The Jordan Times*, December 11, 2013k. As of January 30, 2015:
http://jordantimes.com/ensour-meets-delegates-from-us-rand-corporation

———, "Grace Period for Guest Workers Extended to December 25," *The Jordan Times*, December 21, 2013l. As of January 30, 2015:
http://m.jordantimes.com/grace-period-for-guest-workers-extended-to-december-25

———, "Scores Protest Against Nuclear Project," *The Jordan Times*, December 21, 2013m. As of January 30, 2015:
http://jordantimes.com/scores-protest-against-nuclear-project

———, "Public Health Sector Understaffed—Minister," *The Jordan Times*, December 23, 2013n. As of January 30, 2015:
http://jordantimes.com/public-health-sector-understaffed----minister

———, "Sanitation Worker Jobs to Be Restricted to Jordanian Men, Women," *The Jordan Times*, December 23, 2013o. As of January 30, 2015:
http://cached.newslookup.com/cached.php?ref_id=392&siteid=2317&id=4178413&t=1387857480

———, "Ensour Meets with Women Representatives over Nuclear Project," *The Jordan Times*, December 26, 2013p. As of January 29, 2015:
http://cached.newslookup.com/cached.php?ref_id=392&siteid=2317&id=4205021&t=1388097031

———, "Ensour Discusses Nuclear Project with Heads of Syndicates," *The Jordan Times*, December 28, 2013q. As of January 29, 2015:
http://jordantimes.com/ensour-discusses-nuclear-project-with-heads-of-syndicates

———, "China to Provide Kingdom with Military Equipment Worth $49M," *The Jordan Times*, December 30, 2013r. As of January 28, 2015:
http://jordantimes.com/china-to-provide-kingdom-with-military-equipment-worth-49m

———, "Jordanian Truckers Urged Not to Use Iraqi Border Crossing," *The Jordan Times*, January 7, 2014a. As of January 30, 2015:
http://jordantimes.com/jordanian-truckers-urged-not-to-use-iraqi-border-crossing

———, "EU Grants Jordan 40 Million Euros for Syrian Refugee Crisis," Petra.gov, January 10, 2014b. As of January 30, 2015:
http://www.petra.gov.jo/Public_News/Nws_NewsDetails.aspx?lang=2&site_id=1&NewsID=136070&CatID=13

———, "Japan to Fund Study of Refugee Effect on Water Sector," *The Jordan Times*, January 12, 2014c. As of January 30, 2015:
http://jordantimes.com/japan-to-fund-study-of-refugee-effect-on-water-sector

———, "2,559 Guest Workers Deported in 2013—Katamine," *The Jordan Times*, January 13, 2014d. As of January 30, 2015:
http://jordantimes.com/2559-guest-workers-deported-in-2013----katamine

———, "Unemployment Rate Drops During Last Quarter of 2013," *The Jordan Times*, January 15, 2014e. As of January 30, 2015:
http://jordantimes.com/unemployment-rate-drops-during-last-quarter-of-2013

———, "2,000 Illegal Guest Workers Detained So Far in 2014," *The Jordan Times*, January 26, 2014f. As of January 30, 2015:
http://jordantimes.com/2000-illegal-guest-workers-detained-so-far-in-2014

———, "Jordan's Public Debt Balloons, Topping JD19B," *The Jordan Times*, January 28, 2014g. As of January 30, 2015:
http://jordantimes.com/jordans-public-debt-balloons-topping-jd19b

———, "Syrian Crisis Costs Zarqa City JD2 Million Annually—Mayor," *The Jordan Times*, January 30, 2014h. As of January 30, 2015:
http://jordantimes.com/syrian-crisis-costs-zarqa-city-jd2-million-annually----mayor

———, "Cabinet Approves Recruitment of Syrians," *The Jordan Times*, February 3, 2014i. As of January 30, 2015:
http://jordantimes.com/cabinet-approves-recruitment-of-syrians

"Political Parties, Activists Agree on Plan to Oppose Nuclear Program," *The Jordan Times*, November 10, 2013. As of January 29, 2015:
http://jordantimes.com/political-parties-activists-agree-on-plan-to-oppose-nuclear-programme

"Prices of Eight Food Items Rose by 30% in October—Study," *The Jordan Times*, November 4, 2013. As of January 29, 2015:
http://jordantimes.com/prices-of-eight-food-items-rose-by-30-in-october----study

"Prosecutors to Start Compiling Cases Against Electricity Providers," *The Jordan Times*, December 17, 2013. As of January 29, 2015:
http://jordantimes.com/prosecutors-to-start-compiling-cases-against-electricity-providers

"Protecting Jordan's Higher Interests a Top Priority—King," *The Jordan Times*, January 8, 2014. As of January 29, 2015:
http://jordantimes.com/protecting-jordans-higher-interests-a-top-priority----king

"Protesters Decry Economic Woes," *The Jordan Times*, December 7, 2013. As of January 29, 2015:
http://jordantimes.com/protesters-decry-economic-woes

"Protesters on Friday to Call for PM's Resignation," *The Jordan Times*, November 7, 2013. As of January 29, 2015:
http://jordantimes.com/protesters-on-friday-to-call-for-pms-resignation

Qojas, Mazen, *Cooperative Border Security for Jordan: Assessment and Options*, occasional paper, Albuquerque, N.M.: Sandia National Laboratories, March 1999. As of January 30, 2015:
http://www.sandia.gov/cooperative-monitoring-center/_assets/documents/sand98-05058.pdf

"Radical Cleric Challenges Court Competence, Citing Deal with UK," *The Jordan Times*, December 10, 2013. As of January 29, 2015:
http://jordantimes.com/radical-cleric-challenges-court-competence-citing-deal-with-uk

REACH, *Livelihoods, Employment and Tensions in Jordanian Communities Hosting Syrian Refugees: Thematic Assessment Report*, Amman, Jordan: British Embassy, Amman, June 2014a. As of January 30, 2015:
http://www.reachresourcecentre.info/system/files/resource-documents/reach_jor_report_employmentandtensionsinjordaniancommunitieshostingsyrianrefugees.pdf

———, *Perceptions of External Support in Jordanian Communities Hosting Syrian Refugees: Thematic Assessment Report*, Amman, Jordan: British Embassy, June 2014b. As of January 30, 2015:
http://reliefweb.int/sites/reliefweb.int/files/resources/REACH_JOR_Report_PerceptionsofExternalSupportinJordanianCommunitiesHostingSyrianRefugees.pdf

———, *Syrian Refugees Staying in Informal Tented Settlements in Jordan: Multi-Sector Assessment Report*, Amman, Jordan: UNICEF, June 2014c. As of January 30, 2015:
http://www.reach-initiative.org/wp-content/uploads/2014/09/REACH_UNICEF_ITS_MS_AUGUST2014_FINAL.pdf

———, *Understanding Social Cohesion and Resilience in Jordanian Host Communities: Assessment Report*, Amman, Jordan: British Embassy, June 2014d. As of January 30, 2015:
http://www.reach-initiative.org/wp-content/uploads/2014/06/REACH_Understanding_Social_Cohesion_and_Resilience_in_Jordan_Host_Communities.pdf

"Report: Jordan Closes Its Doors to Hamas Leaders in Solidarity with Egypt," *The Jerusalem Post*, December 17, 2013. As of January 28, 2015:
http://www.jpost.com/Middle-East/Report-Jordan-closes-its-doors-to-Hamas-leaders-in-solidarity-with-Egypt-335308

Reuters, "Jordan Picks Banks for $1.25 Bln U.S.-Guaranteed Sovereign Bond," October 28, 2013a. As of January 30, 2015:
http://www.reuters.com/article/2013/10/28/jordan-bond-idUSL5N0II22720131028

———, "Jordan to Use Gulf Aid to Spur Economy Hit by Syria Crisis," *The Jordan Times*, December 4, 2013b. As of January 30, 2015:
http://jordantimes.com/jordan-to-use-gulf-aid-to-spur-economy-hit-by-syria-crisis

———, "Syrian Opposition Alleges New Poison Gas Attack," *The Jordan Times*, December 7, 2013c. As of January 30, 2015:
http://jordantimes.com/syrian-opposition-alleges-new-poison-gas-attack

Robbins, Michael, and Lawrence Rubin, "The Rise of Official Islam in Jordan," *Politics, Religion and Ideology*, Vol. 14, No. 1, 2013, pp. 59–74.

Robinson, Glenn E., "Can Islamists Be Democrats? The Case of Jordan," *Middle East Journal*, Vol. 51, No. 3, Summer 1997, pp. 373–387.

———, "Defensive Democratization in Jordan," *International Journal of Middle East Studies*, Vol. 30, No. 3, August 1998, pp. 387–410.

"Rosatom Starts Discussion on Construction of Jordan's First Nuclear Power Plant," *Energy Bangla*, February 2, 2014. As of January 28, 2015:
http://energybangla.com/rosatom-starts-discussion-construction-jordan-s-1st-npp/

Ryan, Curtis R., "Peace, Bread, and Riots: Jordan and the International Monetary Fund," *Middle East Policy*, Vol. 6, No. 2, October 1998, pp. 54–66. As of January 30, 2015:
http://libres.uncg.edu/ir/asu/f/Ryan_C_1998_Peace.pdf

———, "Jordanian Foreign Policy and the Arab Spring," *Middle East Policy*, Vol. 21, No. 1, Spring 2014, pp. 144–153.

Saif, Ibrahim, "Impact of Syrian Crisis on Jordan," *The Jordan Times*, January 8, 2014. As of January 30, 2015:
http://jordantimes.com/impact-of-syrian-crisis-on-jordan

Sale, Richard, "Syria's Criminal Gangs," *Al-Monitor*, November 20, 2013. As of January 30, 2015:
http://www.al-monitor.com/pulse/originals/2013/11/syria-terrorist-opposition-atrocities-assad-war.html#

Schwedler, Jillian, "Occupied Maan: Jordan's Closed Military Zone," Washington, D.C.: Middle East Research and Information Project, December 3, 2002. As of January 30, 2015:
http://www.merip.org/mero/mero120302?ip_login_no_cache=e7a5dc263c5a2284a05757454463ab60

"Security Forces Disperse Renewed Port Strike," *The Jordan Times*, December 24, 2013. As of January 29, 2015:
http://jordantimes.com/security-forces-disperse-renewed-port-strike

Serrato, Bryant Castro, *Refugee Perceptions Study: Za'atari Camp and Host Communities in Jordan*, Oxford, UK: Oxfam, 2014.

Shahateet, Mohammed Issa, Fedel Al-Habashneh, and Khalid Ali Al-Majali, "Budget Deficit and External Debt in Jordan: Causality and Co-Integration Analysis," *International Journal of Economics and Finance*, Vol. 6, No. 8, 2014, pp. 268–277.

Sharp, Jeremy M., *Jordan: Background and U.S. Relations*, Washington, D.C.: Congressional Research Service, 2014.

Shihab, Ruba Abu, "The Causal Relationship Between Fiscal Policy and Economic Growth in Jordan," *International Journal of Business and Social Science*, Vol. 5, No. 3, March 2014.

Soffer, Ari, "Jordan: Palestinian Dissident Indicted for Criticizing King," *Arutz Sheva Israel National News*, December 31, 2013. As of January 30, 2015:
http://www.israelnationalnews.com/News/News.aspx/175772#.UswOcfZFeIA

Solomon, Erika, and Laila Bassam, "Jordan Sees Syria Refugee Costs Soar, Vows Subsidy Reform," Reuters, November 15, 2013. As of January 30, 2015:
http://uk.reuters.com/article/2013/11/15/uk-syria-crisis-jordan-minister-idUKBRE9AE0LF20131115

Strategies Policy Research, *Jordan Youth Survey: Universities, Community Colleges and High Schools*, Asian Football Development Project, Amman, Jordan, March 2013.

Su, Alice, "Fade to Black: Jordanian City Ma'an Copes with Islamic State Threat," *Al-Jazeera*, September 2, 2014. As of January 30, 2015:
http://america.aljazeera.com/articles/2014/9/2/jordan-maan-daashthreat.html

"Subsidy Cuts, Higher Housing Costs May Keep Inflation in Jordan High," *The Jordan Times*, January 15, 2014. As of January 29, 2015:
http://jordantimes.com/subsidy-cuts-higher-housing-costs-may-keep-inflation-in-jordan-high

Sullivan, Kathy, "Water from a Stone: Jordanians Stretch Meager Resources to Sustain Syrian Refugees," *Frontlines*, U.S. Agency for International Development, July/August 2013. As of January 30, 2015:
http://www.usaid.gov/news-information/frontlines/aid-action-delivering-results/water-stone-jordanians-stretch-meager

Sundelin, Gaelle, "Water Scarcity Requires Regional, National Cooperation," *The Jordan Times*, October 31, 2013a. As of February 2, 2015:
http://jordantimes.com/water-scarcity-requires-regional-national-cooperation

———, "60–70% of Working Children in Jordan Are Syrians—Ministry," *The Jordan Times*, November 30, 2013b.

———, "Jordan to Turn Back Syrians Coming from Other Countries," *The Jordan Times*, November 25, 2013c.

———, "Syrians Asked to Vacate Informal Tented Settlements, Relocate to Camps," *The Jordan Times*, January 9, 2014.

"Support Platform Set to Endorse National Plan to Address Syrian Crisis," *The Jordan Times*, January 9, 2014. As of January 29, 2015:
http://jordantimes.com/support-platform-set-to-endorse-national-plan-to-address-syrian-crisis

Susser, Asher, "Is the Jordanian Monarchy in Danger?" Crown Center for Middle East Studies, Brief 72, Waltham, Mass.: Brandeis University, April 2013.

Sweis, Rana F., "Brotherhood Leader's Arrest in Jordan Is Seen as Warning from Monarchy," *The New York Times*, December 7, 2014. As of February 2, 2015:
http://www.nytimes.com/2014/12/08/world/brotherhood-leaders-arrest-in-jordan-is-seen-as-warning-from-monarchy.html

Sweis, Rana F., Benjamin Lennett, and Tom Glaisyer, "Spectrum Policy Reforms: Supporting Democracy and Economic Development in Jordan," *Journal of Information Policy*, Vol. 3, 2013, pp. 552–574. As of February 2, 2015:
http://www.jstor.org/stable/10.5325/jinfopoli.3.2013.0552

"Syrian Refugee Services Costing Municipalities $250 Million," *The Jordan Times*, November 3, 2013. As of January 29, 2015:
http://jordantimes.com/syrian-refugee-services-costing-municipalities-250-million

"Syrian Refugees in Jordan: Carefully Watched," *The Economist*, June 18, 2014. As of February 2, 2015:
http://www.economist.com/blogs/pomegranate/2014/06/syrian-refugees-jordan

Taleb, Nassim Nicholas, *The Black Swan: The Impact of the Highly Improbable*, New York: Random House, 2007.

"Terror Suspect Faces All-Civilian Tribunal," *The Jordan Times*, December 24, 2013. As of January 29, 2015:
http://jordantimes.com/terror-suspect-faces-all-civilian-tribunal

Times News Service, "Dar Al Atta'a Lends Help to Syrians," *Times of Oman*, December 30, 2013. As of February 2, 2015:
http://www.timesofoman.com/News/Article-27543.aspx

Udland, Myles, "There Is No Way Around It: These Charts Are Stunning," *Business Insider*, December 12, 2014. As of February 2, 2015:
http://www.businessinsider.com/oil-price-charts-2014-12

UNDP—*See* United Nations Development Programme.

UNHCR—*See* United Nations High Commissioner for Refugees.

"UNHCR to Support Renovation of 5 Bridges in Eastern Border Region," *The Jordan Times*, November 12, 2013. As of January 29, 2015:
http://jordantimes.com/unhcr-to-support-renovation-of-5-bridges-in-eastern-border-region

United Nations Development Programme, "In Jordan, Entrepreneurship Skills Help Weather the Economic Storm," undated. As of February 2, 2015:
http://www.undp.org/content/undp/en/home/ourwork/ourstories/jordan--pulling-yourself-up-by-the-diaper-straps/

———, *Jordan Poverty Reduction Strategy: Final Report*, Amman, Jordan, 2013a.

———, "Mitigating the Impact of the Syrian Refugee Crisis on Jordanian Vulnerable Host Communities," initial survey briefing, 2013b.

———, *Mitigating the Impact of the Syrian Refugee Crisis on Jordanian Vulnerable Host Communities*, report, 2013c.

———, *The Panoramic Study of the Informal Economy in Jordan*, Amman, Jordan, 2013d.

United Nations Development Programme, Jordan Economic and Social Council, and the Spanish Agency for International Development Cooperation, *The Informal Sector in the Jordanian Economy*, Amman, Jordan: Ministry of Planning and International Cooperation, 2010. As of January 28, 2015:
http://inform.gov.jo/en-us/By-Date/Report-Details/ArticleId/34/The-Informal-Sector-in-the-Jordanian-Economy

United Nations High Commissioner for Refugees, "Syrian Refugee Response Tracking," data dashboard, undated. As of February 2, 2015:
http://www.syrianrefugeeresponse.org

———, *UNHCR Policy on Refugee Protection and Solutions in Urban Areas*, policy paper, September 2009.

———, *Syrian Refugees Living Outside Camps in Jordan: Home Visit Data Findings, 2013*, Amman, Jordan, December 2013.

———, *Evaluating the Effect of the Syrian Refugee Crisis on Stability and Resilience in Jordanian Host Communities: Preliminary Impact Assessment*, January 2014a.

———, "End Visit Statement by the United Nations Special Rapporteur on the Human Right to Water and Sanitation, Jordan 11–16 March 2014," United Nations Human Rights, March 16, 2014b. As of February 2, 2015:
http://www.ohchr.org/EN/NewsEvents/Pages/DisplayNews.aspx?NewsID=14386&LangID=E

———, *Syria Regional Refugee Response*, online information portal, data as of July 10, 2014c. As of February 2, 2015:
http://data.unhcr.org/syrianrefugees/regional.php

———, "2014 UNHCR Country Operations Profile—Jordan," web page, data as of July 2014d. As of February 2, 2015:
http://www.unhcr.org/pages/49e486566.html

———, "Jordan," *Syrian Regional Refugee Response*, country page, online information portal, August 25, 2014e. As of February 2, 2015:
http://data.unhcr.org/syrianrefugees/country.php?id=107

———, "Jordan," *Syrian Regional Refugee Response*, country page, online information portal, last updated December 2, 2014f. As of December 2, 2014:
http://data.unhcr.org/syrianrefugees/country.php?id=107

———, *UNHCR Jordan Overview (as of End April, 2014)*, online data pages, 2014g. As of February 2, 2015:
http://www.unhcr.org/4c90819a9.html

United Nations Relief and Works Agency, "Where We Work: Jordan," 2014. As of February 2, 2015:
http://www.unrwa.org/where-we-work/Jordan

United Nations Women, *Gender-Based Violence and Child Protection Among Syrian Refugees in Jordan, with a Focus on Early Marriage*, Amman, Jordan, 2013.

U.S. Agency for International Development, *Evaluating Tax Expenditures in Jordan: Jordan Fiscal Reform II Project*, Amman, Jordan, November 2013. As of February 2, 2015:
http://www.frp2.org/english/Portals/0/PDFs/Technical%20Reports/Evaluating%20Tax%20Expenditures%20in%20Jordan.pdf

USAID—*See* U.S. Agency for International Development.

"USAID to Support Water Reuse Projects in Badia, *The Jordan Times*, December 7, 2013.

U.S. Central Intelligence Agency, *World Fact Book*, Jordan country page, 2014. As of February 2, 2015:
https://www.cia.gov/library/publications/the-world-factbook/geos/jo.html

U.S. Department of State, *Jordan 2013 Crime and Safety Report*, Bureau of Diplomatic Security, January 31, 2013. As of February 2, 2015:
https://www.osac.gov/pages/ContentReportDetails.aspx?cid=13536

———, *Jordan 2014 Crime and Safety Report*, Washington, D.C.: Bureau of Diplomatic Security, May 15, 2014. As of February 2, 2015:
https://www.osac.gov/pages/ContentReportDetails.aspx?cid=15670

U.S. Director of National Intelligence, *Intelligence Community Directive 203: Analytic Standards*, June 21, 2007a. As of January 28, 2015:
http://www.dni.gov/files/documents/ICD/ICD%20203%20Analytic%20Standards%20pdf-unclassified.pdf

———, *Intelligence Community Directive 206: Sourcing Requirements for Disseminated Analytic Products*, October 17, 2007b. As of May 15, 2015:
https://fas.org/irp/dni/icd/icd-206.pdf

Vaida, Petras, "Lithuania and Jordan Discussed Cooperation on Nuclear Safety," *The Baltic Course*, November 21, 2013. As of February 2, 2015:
http://www.baltic-course.com/eng/energy/?doc=83987

Ward, Patricia, "Refugee Cities: Reflections on the Development and Impact of UNHCR Urban Refugee Policy in the Middle East," *Refugee Survey Quarterly*, Vol. 33, No. 1, 2014, pp. 77–93.

We Are All Jordan Forum, *We Are All Jordan—Final Declaration*, Amman, Jordan: Ministry of Planning and International Cooperation, 2006. As of January 27, 2015:
http://inform.gov.jo/en-us/By-Date/Report-Details/ArticleId/16/We-are-all-Jordan-Final-declaration

Wichelns, Dennis, "Virtual Water: A Helpful Perspective, but Not a Sufficient Policy Criterion," *Water Resource Management*, Vol. 24, 2010, pp. 2203–2219.

"Women's Contribution to Economy Barely Increased Since 1993," *The Jordan Times*, January 26, 2014. As of January 29, 2015:
https://www.zawya.com/story/Womens_contribution_to_economy_barely_increased_since_1993-ZAWYA20140127044352/

World Bank, *Jordan—World Bank Country Survey 2013*, December 2013. As of February 2, 2015:
http://microdata.worldbank.org/index.php/catalog/1851

———, "Jordan," web page, 2014. As of February 2, 2015:
http://data.worldbank.org/country/jordan

Yamin, Amjad, "Jordan Third Largest Refugee Host Worldwide—UNHCR," *The Jordan Times*, December 31, 2013. As of February 2, 2015:
http://jordantimes.com/jordan-third-largest-refugee-host-worldwide----unhcr

Yom, Sean L., "The New Landscape of Jordanian Politics: Social Opposition, Fiscal Crisis, and the Arab Spring," *British Journal of Middle Eastern Studies*, 2014a, pp. 1–17.

———, "Tribal Politics in Contemporary Jordan: The Case of the Hirak Movement," *Middle East Journal*, Vol. 68, No. 2, Spring 2014b, pp. 229–247.